Samuel Hallifax

Twelve Sermons on the Prophecies Concerning the Christian Church

and in particular concerning the Church of Papal Rome

Samuel Hallifax

Twelve Sermons on the Prophecies Concerning the Christian Church
and in particular concerning the Church of Papal Rome

ISBN/EAN: 9783337159818

Printed in Europe, USA, Canada, Australia, Japan

Cover: Foto ©Lupo / pixelio.de

More available books at **www.hansebooks.com**

TWELVE SERMONS

ON THE

PROPHECIES

Concerning the CHRISTIAN CHURCH;

AND, IN PARTICULAR,

Concerning the Church of PAPAL ROME:

PREACHED IN LINCOLN'S-INN-CHAPEL,

AT THE LECTURE OF

The Right Reverend WILLIAM WARBURTON
Lord Bishop of GLOUCESTER.

By SAMUEL HALLIFAX, D.D.
Chaplain in Ordinary to His MAJESTY.

LONDON,
PRINTED BY W. BOWYER AND J. NICHOLS:
FOR T. CADELL, IN THE STRAND.
MDCCLXXVI.

TO THE RIGHT HONOURABLE
WILLIAM, Lord MANSFIELD,
LORD CHIEF JUSTICE OF ENGLAND,
AND,
TO THE RIGHT HONOURABLE
Sir JOHN EARDLEY WILMOT, Knt.
LATE LORD CHIEF JUSTICE OF THE
COMMON PLEAS,
TRUSTEES FOR THIS LECTURE,
THE FOLLOWING SERMONS
ARE MOST HUMBLY INSCRIBED
BY THE AUTHOR,

S. HALLIFAX.

CAMBRIDGE,
MARCH 13, 1776.

CONTENTS.

SERMON I.

The Truth of Revealed Religion, in general, and of the Christian, in particular, proved from Prophecy.

REV. iii. 22.

He that hath an ear, let him hear what the Spirit saith unto the Churches. page 1.

SERMON II.

The Authority of the Book of Daniel.

DANIEL xii. 10.

None of the wicked shall understand; but the wise shall understand. p. 32.

SERMON III.

Prophecies of Daniel concerning the Four Empires.

DANIEL ii. 44.

And in the days of these Kings shall the God of heaven set up a Kingdom, which shall never be destroyed. p. 66.

SERMON IV.

Prophecies of Daniel concerning Antiochus Epiphanes and Antichrist.

DANIEL xiii. 8, 9.

Then said I, O my Lord, What shall be the End of these things? And he said, Go thy way, Daniel; for the words are closed up and sealed, till the time of the End. p. 99.

CONTENTS.

SERMON V.

Prophecy of St. Paul concerning the Man of Sin.

2 THESS. ii. 3.

Let no man deceive you by any means: for That Day shall not come, except there come a falling-away first, and that Man of Sin be revealed, the Son of Perdition. p. 133.

SERMON VI.

Prophecy of St. Paul concerning the Apostasy of the Latter Times.

1 TIMOTHY iv. 1.

Now the Spirit speaketh expressly, that in the Latter Times some shall depart from the Faith; giving heed to seducing spirits, and Doctrines of Devils. p. 166.

CONTENTS.

SERMON VII.

The Authority of the Apocalypse, and the Time when it was written.

REV. i. 3.

Blessed is he that readeth, and they that hear, the words of this prophecy, and keep those things which are written therein; for the time is at hand.   p. 193.

SERMON VIII.

The Order and Connexion of the Visions of the Apocalypse.

REV. i. 19.

Write the things which thou hast seen, and the things which Are, and the things which Shall Be Hereafter.   p. 226.

SERMON IX.

Vision of the Apocalypse concerning the Babylonish Woman.

REV. xvii. 18.

The Woman, which thou sawest, is that Great

CONTENTS.

Great City which reigneth over the kings of the earth.   p. 261.

SERMON X.

General Design of the remaining Visions of the Apocalypse.

REV. xxii. 6.

These sayings are faithful and true; and the Lord God of the holy prophets sent his Angel, to shew unto his servants the things which must shortly be done. p. 290.

SERMON XI.

Historical View of the Corruptions of Popery.

ACTS xxvi. 22.

Saying none other things than those, which the Prophets—did say should come. p. 328.

SER-

SERMON XII.

The Reformation vindicated from the objections of the Romanists. Conclusion.

Rev. xviii. 4.

Come out of her, my people; that ye be not partakers of her sins, and that ye receive not of her plagues. p. 363.

SERMON I.

The Truth of Revealed Religion, in general, and of the Christian, in particular, proved from Prophecy.

Rev. iii. 22.
He that hath an ear, let him hear what the Spirit saith unto the Churches.

A REVELATION, which claims to come from God, besides the internal arguments of its divinity, arising from its Doctrines, ought also to be accompanied with the external proofs of MIRACLES and PROPHECIES. Of these we are to conceive, not as intended for the benefit and conviction of the same persons and times, but as providently accommodated to the wants of different ages, and given in succession. On the first publication of a new religion, there is an evident necessity in the nature of the thing, not only that the Doctrines be such as, for their reasonableness and importance, are worthy of God to communicate, but also, that the immediate publishers of this religion be enabled to attest the reality of their mission by MIRACLES. Neither doctrines alone, nor miracles alone, are a sufficient testimony, that the revelation containing them is divine. The *lying wonders* [a], fabricated in Pagan and even in Christian times, to support the labouring interests of vice and superstition, are an ample proof that the most specious miracles, of themselves, are no security from fraud and error. Again, we cannot with certainty infer that doctrines, confessedly worthy of God to reveal, did indeed, in an extraordinary way, descend

[a] 2 Thess. ii. 9.

from him; becaufe we know not, with exactnefs, the precife limits of the human underftanding, or what truths there may be, however remote from vulgar apprehenfion, which by a well-directed application of its own powers it is capable of difcovering. But when a perfon, affuming to be an infpired meffenger, delivers with authority a fyftem of religious belief and practice, which is plainly calculated to promote the glory of God and the prefent and future good of mankind; and, in confirmation of fo fublime a character, is able to arreft and fufpend the laws of nature by the production of that effect we call a Miracle; in fuch a cafe, we may fafely repofe on the veracity and goodnefs of God, that the wonderful works of one fo circumftanced are neither the artful machinations of wicked men, nor the more dangerous delufions of wicked fpirits; but were purpofely wrought in order to bear witnefs to his words, and to afford a fenfible demonftration,

tion, that he is indeed *a teacher come from God; for no man could do* those *miracles* which he does, *except God were with him* [b].

The same reasons, which shew the necessity of Miracles on the first promulgation of a new religion, serve also to shew that, when once this end is answered, the power of them should be withdrawn. Extraordinary appearances of this kind are never indulged in vain; and whenever they have been allowed, it hath always been with a frugal hand, and a parsimonious liberality. They are fitted by their novelty, as well as by the authority implied in the performers of them, to rouse the attention of mankind for a time: but this attention would be weakened, in proportion as the novelty diminished; when grown to be familiar, and viewed without surprize, they would be no more regarded than the standing monuments of divine power, exhibited every day in the works of creation and providence; be-

[b] John iii. 2.

sides that so frequent a violation of the course of nature, as is supposed in the constant display of them, would be inconsistent with an established order and government of the world.

Nor would any inconvenience be felt by the ceasing of this celestial gift, if, immediately or soon after its subduction, what was mentioned above as the second external proof of Revelation were now introduced, the word of PROPHECY. This, which in the age of Miracles was not wanted, and might therefore well be spared, is, on the discontinuance of that supernatural endowment, an adequate compensation for its loss. Miracles, after being once wrought, partake so far of the nature of other past facts, as only to be verified on the authority of human testimony; an authority which, by length of time, is liable to become more and more imperfect, and subject to continual weakness and decay. But the argument from Prophecy preserves its force through a course

course of ages, unimpaired; and like the light which gilds the approaches of the morning, shines with encreasing lustre the further we advance from the time of its discovery. The reason is, Prophecies are not, as Miracles, unrelated to and independent of one another; but are to be considered as constituting a Whole or System, whose parts are mutually connected, and all refer to one consistent design, determined beforehand even to the minutest circumstance in the counsels of providence, and uniformly pursued through a series of succeeding generations, and opened with proportionably greater degrees of perspicuity, as the time for its full completion draweth near. Hence it follows, that the scheme of prophecy is not confined to one age, begun and ended, as it were, at once; but distributed through a long tract of time, and fulfilled gradually, and after certain intervals: by which *springing and germinant accomplishment,*

ment, as Lord Bacon calls it [c], every single prediction, when sorted with the event, becomes in its turn a new confirmation of the faith; and the latter ages of the world have as fresh and forcible means of conviction as the former. Thus these two pillars of Revelation, though distinct in themselves, and either of them alone sufficient, are made, when disposed by the plastic hand of the Almighty Architect, to contribute to the support and ornament of each other; and the traditional and still weakening authority of Miracles is upheld by the *more sure* [d] and growing evidence of Prophecy. Each proof, in its way, is peculiarly adapted to the times and persons, for whose benefit it was intended; and both together form a complete and conclusive argument for the truth of that dispensation which contains them.

To apply what has now been said on revealed religion, in general, to the

[c] Advancement of Learning, book ii.
[d] 2 Pet. i. 19.

SERM. I.

Jewish and Christian religions, in particular.

I. The JEWISH LAW, though it had indeed a *relative* perfection, namely that of attaining its end, which was, to preserve alive among a people, purposely separated from the rest of the nations, the doctrine of One living and true God; carried along with it the most unequivocal marks, interwoven into its constitution, that it was never intended by its divine author to be a general law for mankind, nor to be of perpetual obligation even to the Jews. The better to secure this separation during the time it was to last, a form of government was instituted, singular in its nature, and without example among the varying polities of the world, a Theocracy; in which God himself condescended to be the Magistrate of this favoured people, and exercised all those acts of sovereignty, which were proper to convince them they were the real and immediate subjects of his kingdom. From hence

hence it appears, that the interpoſition of the Supreme Being, which was viſible for ſo long a period, in the conduct of the civil and religious concerns of the Jews, was but a neceſſary conſequence of the peculiar form of their polity; or, in other words, that it was of the eſſence of a government, like that we are now contemplating, that it ſhould be adminiſtered by Miracles and Prophecies. Miracles were abſolutely requiſite, to execute the temporal rewards and puniſhments, annexed to the Law: and Prophecy, by declaring beforehand the ſucceſſes and calamities that were to happen to the Jewiſh ſtate, were a never-failing ſource of truſt and confidence, as well to them who heard the predictions delivered as to thoſe who ſaw them fulfilled, that all the great affairs of this republic were under the direction of an unerring guide, who *declareth the end from the beginning, and from ancient times the things that are not yet done, ſaying,*

saying, My counsel shall stand, and I will do all my pleasure[e].

But Prophecy, in the manner it was imparted to this nation, served another and yet sublimer use. The religion of Moses, we have said, was to last but for a time, and to prepare the way for a more perfect institution, to be delivered by Jesus, which should be the completion, or, if you will, the extension of that which preceded. There being then this dependency between the two religions, it is reasonable to suppose that, previous to such an important change of the œconomy, some intimations should be given of its approach. And yet to have done this in a way, that would have led the Jews to look with irreverence on a system, under which not only themselves but their posterity were to live, would have been little agreeable to our notions of the divine wisdom. A method therefore was to be invented, which, whilst it

[e] If. xlvi. 10.

kept

kept the people sincerely addicted to the Law, should dispose them, when the time was come, for the reception of a *better covenant*, that should be *established upon better promises*[f]. Now the spirit of Prophecy, together with the Language in which that prophecy was conveyed, fully accomplished both these purposes. By a contrivance, only to be suggested by divine prescience, the same expressions, which, in their primary and literal meaning, were used to denote the fortunes and deliverances of the Jews, for the present consolation of that people, were so ordered, as, in a secondary and figurative sense, to adumbrate the sufferings and victories of the Messiah, for the future instruction of the church of Christ. Had no expedient of this sort been employed, we should have wanted *one* proof of the connection between the Mosaic and Christian religions: on the other hand, had the nature of the Messiah's kingdom

[f] Heb. viii. 6.

been

been *plainly* described, the design of the national separation would have been defeated. But when spiritual blessings were promised, under the veil of temporal, and in terms familiar to the carnal expectations of the Jews; a proper degree of respect for the old system was preserved, at the same time that matters were gradually ripening for the introduction of the new; and *the shadow of good things*, held forth obscurely in the Law, prepared them to look forward to that happier day, when the *very image* [g] itself should be presented, in full splendor, and distinctly defined, in the Gospel.

From the delineation here given of the religious œconomy of the Jews, it appears that their civil regimen, on account of the singular mode of providence by which it was conducted, had the force of a continued *Miracle:* and their Law, on account of its spiritual meaning, partook of the

[g] Heb. x. i.

nature

nature of *Prophecy*. Nor does this oppose what was said before concerning these two fundamental proofs of Revelation, that they should be raised in succession: for we are here to observe that the Miracles, recorded in the Jewish history, are of two sorts [h]; the one were wrought to evince the truth and divine original of the Mosaic religion; the other were incorporated into its frame and structure, to support it after its establishment, and by way of distributing the rewards and punishments, which constituted the sanction of the Law: the intent of the former was satisfied, when once the authority of the new religion was confirmed; the latter were essentially connected with the extraordinary administration, and ceased together with it, on the

[h] See *A free and candid Examination of the principles of the Bishop of London's Sermons*, etc. London, 1756. Chap. v. where this distinction, and the uses to be served by it, are explained at large, with a penetration and acuteness peculiar to the Examiner.

return

return of the Jews from their captivity. So did not Prophecy; which was carried on, in one unbroken chain, to the end of this republic; nor ever intermitted of its operation, till it had precisely marked out, what indeed was its principal object to ascertain, the advent of that Illustrious Person, whom it uniformly describes under every dispensation, though in a manner adapted to the genius of each, as the destined restorer of the human race to that immortality which had been forfeited by the fall, and fore-ordained to become *the author of eternal salvation to* ALL *that obey him*[i], whether Jews or Gentiles. Nor can any adequate cause be assigned for what we know to have been an undoubted fact, the universal *expectation* of some great prophet; which prevailed throughout the East, at the very period, when Jesus appeared in Judæa; unless such an expectation be ascribed to the authority of prophecy, and especially to the prophe-

[i] Heb. v. 9.

cies

cies to be found in the book of Daniel[k]: in which the coming of the Messiah is foretold to happen, not only in general, within the times of the fourth, or Roman, kingdom; but more particularly, within a given term of years after the restoration of the city of Jerusalem, then desolated by the Babylonish captivity, and before the destruction of the Jewish temple and government. There is not the least colour for asserting, that the numerous predictions of this sort, delivered at different times and by different men, were written after the event; nor can it be pretended they were, all of them, fulfilled in the history of any other person but that of Jesus. What remains then but that we admit, what the whole tenor of scripture authorizes us to conclude, that they were designedly given to erect the minds of thoughtful men towards a future and

---

[k] Dan. ii. 44, 45. vii. 23. ix. 24—27. See *Bp. Chandler's* Defence of Christianity, ch. i. and ii. where this matter is considered at large.

more

more enduring system, at the time their own was going to decay, and to comfort them with the hopes of better days to come?.

II. The Christian Religion, being neither temporary in its nature, nor appropriated to the uses of one people, but calculated for perpetual duration and the general benefit of mankind, has not experienced those frequent interventions of an extraordinary providence, nor that variety of successive prophecies, which were vouchsafed to the Jews. The power of miracles, granted at first as the credential of the new revelation, lasted no longer than the time of its firm establishment; and the prophetic spirit was wholly confined to the persons of Christ and his Apostles, particularly St. Paul and St. John. Nor will such a display of divine goodness, in support of this its last and best dispensation, be thought too penurious; if we reflect that an ample provision was made for producing, both in the primitive

mitive and present times, the fullest demonstration of its truth. If the proof from Miracles be properly addressed to those only, who saw the wonders performed; and to others, who are removed from the scene of action, becomes less and less satisfactory; the argument from Prophecy remains unhurt amidst all the ravages of time, and every increase of its age is but a new addition to its strength. As the predictions in the New Testament have some of them had their completion, and others will remain to be fulfilled, to the final consummation of all things; there is room for a continual accession of evidence, in favour of the divine original of Christianity, to the last period of the world: till at length, as we are taught by our inspired oracles to expect, the conviction, arising from its accumulated force, will grow to such a height, that no obstacle, whether of vice or error, shall be able to stand before it; the *veil*, which *blindeth the minds of them that believe*

lieve not, and intercepts their right apprehension of the ways and works of God, shall be completely *done away*¹; and, Jews and Gentiles being now converted to the same faith, *the kingdoms of this world* shall *become the kingdoms of our Lord and of his Christ, and he shall reign for ever and ever* ᵐ.

Add to this, that the temporal deliverances, promised to the Israelites under the Law, were all of them *typical* of the spiritual blessings to be conferred by the Gospel; though the knowledge of such blessings could not be openly declared, without anticipating the time, allotted to that preparatory system. When these predictions, in their direct and obvious acceptation, were made good, in the civil occurrences of the Jews; they became so many *pledges* and *assurances*, that they would hereafter be accomplished, in their more sublime and secret meaning: and

¹ 2 Cor. iv. 4. and iii. 14.
ᵐ Rev. ii. 15.

when

when again this remote and myſtical ſenſe was verified in the perſon and religion of Jeſus; ſuch a *double* completion was a ſtriking argument that, under the old covenant as well as the new, the hopes of eternal life were founded on a Redeemer, coming or come; the efficacy of whoſe merits was to extend to all the deſcendants of Adam, whether born before or after his manifeſtation; and who, in alluſion to this retroſpective virtue of his death, is called *the Lamb ſlain from the foundation of the world* [n].

III. I have detained you thus long on the general ſubject of Miracles and Prophecies, and in explaining the manner, in which theſe were applied, in proof of the two diſpenſations of Judaiſm and Chriſtianity; in order to introduce, with greater advantage, what I have now to offer concerning the Prophecies, which *relate to the Chriſtian church.* Theſe, whether obſcurely delivered by the legal prophets,

[n] Rev. xiii. 8.

or more clearly revealed by the evangelical, have been conveniently diftributed under two heads: they either relate to the *perfonal character of Chrift*, or to *the fortunes of his religion*. Of the former fort are the predictions in the Old and New Teftament, in which are foretold the birth and life, the fufferings and death, the refurrection and afcenfion of the Meffiah: with other circumftances, beyond the fagacity of human forefight to conjecture, or human power to bring to pafs; which yet, in the hiftory of Jefus, have been punctually fulfilled. The prophecies of the latter clafs are thofe, which demand our efpecial confideration in the prefent Lecture.

Of thefe there are two, which, as containing in brief the different fates of both the religions above defcribed, deferve to be particularly noticed. The firft is that which concerns *the deftruction of the City and Temple of Jerufalem*: and its importance may be thus conceived. From the

the flighteft attention to the order of the divine œconomy it appears, that the Law and the Gofpel, though nearly related and dependent fyftems, were never defigned to exift together; and that the abolition of the Mofaic religion was of neceffity to precede the perfect eftablifhment of the Chriftian. Now it was an exprefs command in the Hebrew ritual, that the ceremonies and facrifices, there prefcribed, fhould only be performed in one determined place; and that place, after the times of Solomon, it is agreed, was the Temple at Jerufalem. So long therefore as the Temple fubfifted, Judaifm was permitted to remain in force: when that was deftroyed, the local worfhip, and the religious inftitution founded on it, were deftroyed alfo. But a revolution fo fingular as this, and which, whenever it happened, was to be followed by nothing lefs than the total fubverfion of the Jewifh polity, it is natural to expect, would not be fuffered to efcape the folemn notice

notice of prophecy; and accordingly we find it announced, firſt, indefinitely and at large, by Daniel [o], and then again, and with greater minuteneſs, by Jeſus [p]. The proofs of the accompliſhment of this prediction are almoſt as remarkable as the prediction itſelf, and are furniſhed by a writer, whoſe teſtimony in this caſe is above ſuſpicion. Joſephus, a Jew and a Prieſt, who was himſelf a ſharer in the calamities of his countrymen, has deſcribed, in detail, the ſeveral particulars that attended the ſiege of the city and temple, as it was effected by the Roman armies, under the conduct of Titus. His hiſtory and our Lord's prophecy, compared together, mutually explain and illuſtrate each other; and produce in well-diſpoſed minds ſuch a perſuaſion concerning the general truth of the Goſpel, as cannot be reſiſted. The ancient Chriſti-

[o] Dan. ix. 26, 27.
[p] Matth. xxiv. Mark xiii. Luke xvii. 20—37. and ch. xxi.

ans were wont to contemplate the matter in this view, and to infist on fo fignal an inftance of the divine fore-knowledge of Jefus as an irrefragable argument that He was the Chrift. And when, in after-times, an Apoftate Emperor attempted, at an immenfe expence, to rebuild the Temple, on purpofe to falfify the prophecies, which had foretold its final defolation; the honour of God's decrees was openly vindicated with all the tokens of incenfed omnipotence; and balls of fire, burfting out from the foundation, repelled the blafted workmen from daring to reftore its ruins[q].

Another prophecy, intimately connected with the foregoing, and of equal importance in the hiftory of the Chriftian Church, is that which refpects the *conversion of the Heathen nations to the faith of Chrift.* When the revelation of Jefus

---

[q] See the Difcourfe entitled *Julian*; where the reality of this Miracle is fatisfactorily proved, by the very learned Founder of this Lecture.

was first proposed to mankind, not content with being simply admitted by its followers as *true*, it required still further that they should embrace it as the *only true one*; the consequence of which was, it could no otherwise be established, but on the ruin or abolition of every other religion. The various and contradictory doctrines of Pagan theology it formally condemned of falshood; and though it owned the truth and divinity of Judaism, and even professed to be built on it, as its foundation, yet it contended that the law of Moses was now to be abrogated, and that, having gained its end in preserving the memory of One God till the coming of the Messiah, it was no longer binding on those to whom it was addressed. Such pretensions were not likely to conciliate the affections either of Jews or Gentiles: the former, with the utmost abhorrence of every other institution, and fatally persuaded of the *absolute* perfection of their own, thought no persons

sons worthy of the protection of heaven but themselves: and the latter, accustomed to an intercommunity of worship, and strangers to the idea of an *universal* religion, were averse to allow the claims of one, which refused to be received but on the destruction of the rest. With this unpromising prospect, the blessed Jesus, now about to withdraw from his disciples, gave them his last command to *go into all the world, and preach the gospel to every creature*[r]: at the same time, lest they should be discouraged from the attempt, he expressly told them, that, in spite of every obstacle, their endeavours should be followed with success, and the work of the Lord should prosper in their hands. The event was every way conformable to the prediction. In opposition to the obstinacy of superstition, the pride of philosophy, and the violence of civil power, the religion of Christ gradually made its way, and in the compass of three hundred

[r] Mark xvi. 15.

hundred years became the religion of the world. Much, no doubt, still remains to be done, ere this great design of providence be brought to its perfection: but the same spirit of prophecy, which once declared that, before the *generation* of men then living should *pass away, the gospel should be preached for a witness to all nations* [s], hath also predicted, that the days will come, when its dominion shall be strictly Universal; when *darkness* shall no more *cover the earth,* nor *gross darkness the people* [t]; and the *consummation,* spoken of by Daniel, and *the times of the Gentiles,* as that word is interpreted by Christ, *shall* at length *be* happily *fulfilled* [u].

The two prophecies, which have here been offered to your consideration, are among the most illustrious of those, which relate to the Christian Church; and having both received their completion, they

[s] Matth. xxiv. 14, 34.
[t] Is. lx. 2.
[u] Dan. ix. 27. Luke xxi. 24.

become direct and positive proofs of the divinity of our religion. To have discussed them with the care and accuracy they deserve, would have exceeded the limits of my intended plan; and would *now*, for a reason that need not be mentioned, have been unnecessary [w]. Yet even this slight and perfunctory examination may have its use, in preparing you for what is next to solicit your patient hearing, through the following Lectures, the prophecies in the Old and New Testament, which describe the *Apostasy of Papal Rome.* It is doubtless to be lamented by those who are engaged in this argument, that the governing principle, by which it is to be supported, and which was formerly held as the common symbol of Protestantism, namely—That the Pope or Church of Rome is the Antichrist, whose character and fortunes are foretold in those predictions—should have fallen into dis-

---

[w] See the Sixth of Bp. Hurd's Sermons on the Prophecies.

repute: and particularly, that a man, so supremely skilled in the nature of moral evidence as the great Lord Chancellor Clarendon, should have regarded it, as some *judgement* on those who have pretended to make the discovery, (which, he asserts, may as reasonably be applied to *any other person whom they do not love*) that, *being many of them in other arguments men of parts and clear ratiocination, they no sooner entered and exercised themselves in this, than they immediatly became perplext and obscure, that their nearest friends could not understand them*[x]. Thus this great man; crudely and inconsiderately, indeed; but according to the sentiments and language of his time. The present age, it may be hoped, among its other attainments in religious knowledge, is destined to restore the credit of an opinion, which in the sixteenth century was

[x] See his Miscellaneous Works, in one Volume, Folio; and the last of the *Essays, Against the multiplying Controversies*, &c. p. 259.

thought

thought alone sufficient to justify the separation from the Church of Rome, and may still, we think, be shewn to have a real foundation in Scripture. To promote so desirable an end, to vindicate the truth and purity of Reformed Religion, is the simple purpose of this Protestant Lecture. The philosopher, who has habituated himself to scoff at all revelation, may laugh at our mistaken pains to preserve the integrity of the Christian; or even deride the attempt, as no better than the dotage of a disordered understanding: the man of the world, immersed in the indulgencies of sense, or eager in the pursuits of ambition, may be little disposed to attend to an argument, that might detain him too long from his wonted gratifications: and the papist, accustomed to repose under the venerable shade of authority, may have his reasons for representing us, as influenced by prudential motives and a political aversion, when we would fix the brand of Antichrist on the Roman Pontiff.

Pontiff. In the mean while, the sober and difpaffionate enquirer; *he that hath an ear*, purged from the feculence of vice, and cleanfed from the impurities of fuperftition; fuch a one will not be hafty in leffening the merits of an inftitution, which, if founded on truth, muft be allowed to concern us, in the higheft degree, both as Chriftians and Proteftants; at leaft will not affect to treat it with contempt and ridicule, till he hath arrived at the moft deliberate conviction of its futility. For though to interpret prophecies before they are fulfilled, be an attempt that is often dangerous, and always prefumptuous; to illuftrate thofe, whofe meaning is now explained by the event; to admire and adore the hand, which is not more confpicuous in the prediction than the completion; is furely, if any, an endeavour that may conduce to the moft effential interefts of revealed religion. It is to this point only, that our future fpeculations are to be directed; and now we are

are entering on so august a theme, I cannot better bespeak your attention than in those awful words, so emphatically repeated, in the Gospels and in the book of the Revelation, by him, who is the *Alpha and Omega, the beginning and end* y *of* prophecy, *He that hath an ear, let him hear what the Spirit saith unto the Churches* z.

y Rev. xxii. 13.
z Rev. ch. ii. 7, 11, 27, 29. Ch. iii. 6, 13, 22. Ch. xiii. 9.

SERMON II.

The Authority of the Book of DANIEL.

DANIEL xii. 10.

None of the wicked shall understand; but the wise shall understand.

SERM. II.

THE predictions, which respect the state of the Christian Church, under the usurpation of a certain tyrannical power, commonly known by the name of Antichrist, and which, as we say, are to be interpreted of Papal Rome, are contained in the book of Daniel, in two Epistles of St. Paul, and in the Revelation of St. John. Of these the first in order

of

of time, and of principal confideration in the prefent Lecture, is Daniel. His prophecies make up the clue, which was afterwards evolved, diftinctly and at length, by the writers who fucceeded him. It was in confequence of what had been foretold by him concerning the 70 weeks, or 490 years, allotted for the continuance of the Jewifh city and fanctuary, after each had been reftored on the return of that people from captivity [a], that the coming of the Meffiah, towards the end of that period, was generally expected among the nations of the Eaft. To the fame prediction, as of allowed authority, and with a particular caution that he who *reads* fhould *underftand* it, our Lord refers, in his own denunciation of the then impending ruin of the Temple of Jerufalem; who alfo takes efpecial care to diftinguifh him by the title of *Prophet* [b]. St. Paul's defcription of the

[a] Dan. ix. 24—27.
[b] Matth. xxiv. 15.

Apostacy of *the latter times* is at once prefaced and confirmed by what *the Spirit* had *expressly spoken* before, by the mouth of Daniel[c]. In the Apocalypse of St. John, the same events, and persons, and times are treated of, the same symbols and images, the same style and colouring are adopted, as had been used by the legal prophet: as might naturally be expected in the works of two persons, both inspired by the same Spirit, both represented in Scripture as peculiarly dear to God[d], and both employed in revealing, for the conviction of future ages, a regular chain of events, from the beginning of the Jewish captivity to that awful period, when all the purposes of God to man shall be finally completed at the day of judgement. The religion of Christ being thus evidently founded on what had been declared by Daniel concerning the Messiah,

---

[c] 1 Tim. iv. 1.

[d] Dan. ix. 23. and x. 11. John xiii. 23. xix. 26. xx. 2. xxi. 7. 20. 24.

it was not without reason affirmed by the great Sir Isaac Newton, that *to reject his Prophecies is to reject the Christian Religion*[e]. He who owns the authority of one can have no scruples about admitting the truth of the other; and the adversaries of Daniel and of Christianity, from Porphyry down to Collins, have always been the same.

Before we enter on the consideration of the predictions of the Jewish prophet, it may be proper, for the sake of those, who may think such a previous enquiry to be but necessary, to observe to you what hath been urged by learned men, professedly engaged on this subject, in proof of the *Authenticity of the Book itself*.

I. And the first thing, that takes our attention in this remarkable composition is, that one part of it is *Prophetical*, and the other is *Historical*. The six first chapters are chiefly of the Historic class; the

[e] Sir I. Newton's Observations on the Prophecies. Part i. ch. iii.

SERM. II.

second only containing a prophecy of *what should be in the latter days*[f]: the six last chapters are all Prophetical, and, being written in the first person, were probably the work of Daniel himself. With regard to that part which is Historical, I do not know, that a defender of Prophecy is more concerned to prove the authority of this than of any other book of Scripture: indeed not so much; as it is easy to conceive, in the present instance, that the History may have been adulterated, and yet the Prophecies been preserved sincere. In other cases, Histories are generally the compilement of one writer, comprehending a series of past transactions, delivered in chronological order, and usually carrying their own evidence either of truth or falshood along with them: but the book in question, on the face of it, is of a very different complexion; the Historical part, which is comprised in the former half, being none

[f] Dan. ii. 28.

of it put together by Daniel, and almost all of it completed after his death. It is a known thing, that several narrations, of the Historic sort, have been ascribed to this prophet, which, it is now agreed, were nothing better than forgeries of some later Jews: such were the Song of the three Children, the stories of Bel and of Susannah, all formerly inserted into the third chapter, in the Greek language, although never admitted into the Hebrew copies. Not that any advantage can fairly be made of this concession, as if that part of the book, which was all along received into the Jewish canon, were fabulous: on the contrary, it hath been proved, and to the satisfaction of fair enquirers, to abound with all the marks of genuine antiquity. The reputation for wisdom, which Daniel is reported to have acquired at Babylon, is confirmed by the testimony of Ezekiel, his fellow captive there [g]; and the same author, on another

[g] Ezek. xxviii. 3.

occasion, ranks him with Noah and Job, as eminent examples of piety [h]. His own deliverance from the lions, and that of his countrymen from the fiery furnace [i], are mentioned, among other instances taken from Scripture, by the writer of the first book of the Maccabees [k]; above two centuries after the age of Daniel, and almost as many before the coming of Christ. What can be more natural than the account, given in the first and following chapters, of the education and fortunes of this extraordinary person? that he was brought up, with other captive youths, in the court of the king of Babylon; that, because *an excellent spirit was found in him* [l], he was raised to the honour of being the first of the three Ministers of the Empire [m]; and afterwards, through the malice of his adver‑

[h] Ezek. xiv. 14. 20.
[i] Dan. ch. vi. and ch. iii.
[k] 1 Macc. ii. 59, 60.
[l] Dan. v. 11, 12.
[m] Dan. v. 29. vi. 2, 3.

faries, envious that a stranger should be preferred before them, was exposed to the most imminent danger, from which nothing but the arm of heaven, visibly stretched out in defence of its chosen servant, could have rescued him [n]. What can better describe the usual workings of instant terror and inveterate habits, than the conduct of the idolatrous princes of Babylon and Media; who are represented as acknowleging the superiority of the God of the Jews, and as it were in haste to engage his protection, when impressed with the recent sense of his power and providence; and then again, on the removal of their first alarm, returning with equal speed to their wonted superstitions [o]? Or what more agreeable to the relations of other historians concerning the uncontroulable genius of Asiatic despotism, than the description of the *Law of the Medes and Persians*; that, when once issued by the king, it was regarded by his

[n] Ch. vi.   [o] Ch. iii. and vi.

subjects, and even by himself, as resistless as the course of nature, and like that incapable of change and alteration [p]? In a word, the stile and turn of the whole performance accord so exactly with the situation of the supposed author; his characters are so well preserved; the customs alluded to, whether of Jews or Pagans, correspond so justly with the times; and each incident is so peculiarly accommodated to the occasion that brought it forth; as, all together, to amount to a very high degree of presumptive evidence, in favour of the authenticity of this sacred composition.

If there be any circumstance, in which the veracity of the writer seems to labour, it is that which respects the names of the Kings, whom he affirms to have reigned in Babylon and Persia. But out of four mentioned by him, in the first and the last, *Nebuchadnezzar* and *Cyrus* [q], it is con-

[p] Dan. vi. 8. 12. 15.
[q] Ch. i. 1. 21. vi. 28.

fessed, there is no mistake. The second, *Belshazzar*[r], is indeed denominated otherwise by the Greek Historians; who yet are observed to differ from one another as much as they do from Daniel; Herodotus calling him by one name, Megasthenes by another, Berosus by a third, Josephus by a fourth. It was a common practice in the East, as we learn from sacred and profane history, for the more celebrated of their personages to be distinguished by a multitude of appellations: even to Daniel and his three companions new names are said to have been assigned by the chief of the eunuchs, who belonged to Nebuchadnezzar[s]. The prophet, who resided in the courts of Babylon and Persia, could not be ignorant of the names of any of his royal masters; nor would the author, had he lived so late as is pretended, have hazarded his credit

---

[r] Dan. v. 1. 30. vii. 1.
[s] Ch. i. 7. iv. 8. v. 12.

by inserting the name of a king, which was known to no historian but himself.

But the greatest difficulty of all is in the third king, said here to be *Darius the Mede*[t]. It is certain, no prince of this name or nation, between the times of Nebuchadnezzar and Cyrus, is to be found in the series of the Babylonian and Persian dynasties, whether fetched from the canon of Ptolemy, or the fragments of Berosus; and, on the first view, it appears no easy matter to account for such an omission, so as to save the honour of the inspired penman. Among the many expedients, invented with this design, there is one which hath been followed by the ablest of our chronologers, and seems every way qualified for the purpose, which is this; that the Darius of Daniel, and the Cyaxares of Xenophon, are one and the same person. This prince, the second of his name, was uncle, and afterwards father-in-law, to Cyrus the king of Persia; and

[t] v. 31. vi. 28. ix. 1.

son to Astyages, whom he succeeded in the throne of Media. The better to ascertain his identity with Darius, it is supposed, that after the city of Babylon was taken by Cyrus, and with all the circumstances foretold, with such astonishing particularity, by Isaiah and Jeremiah [u], the *nominal* sovereignty of that kingdom, by permission of the conqueror, was vested in Cyaxares, for the remainder of his life; and that it was not till the event of his death, which happened *two years afterwards*, that the *whole* command devolved entirely on Cyrus. This hypothesis, which is probable in itself, is not incompatible with the received chronology, and consents, in perfect concord, with the book of Daniel: where we read, that *Darius the Median* was *about threescore and two years old*, when he *took the kingdom* of Babylon [w], on the death of Belshazzar; and where officious pains are

[u] If. ch. xiii. xiv. xlvi. xlvii. Jer. ch. l. li.
[w] Dan. v. 31.

used to mark the dates of the prophetical visions, some of them as seen in the *first* year of Darius, and others in the *third* year of Cyrus king of Persia[x]. As to the silence of the Greek writers, who make Cyrus the *immediate* successor to Astyages in the kingdom of Media, without the intervention of any such person either as Darius or Cyaxares; the Persians, from whom the Greeks had their relation, would naturally be disposed to ascribe the whole merit of so important a conquest to their countryman; and, it being on all hands agreed that the siege of Babylon was *chiefly* effected by him, during the absence of Cyaxares, the fame of the Median prince might easily be lost in the reputation of his royal nephew. However, Josephus, forsaking in this instance his oracle Berosus, whom in other respects he is prone to follow, expressly asserts, not only that Babylon was destroyed by the forces of Cyrus and Darius in conjunction,

[x] Dan. ix. 1. xi. 1. x. 1.

The Authority of the Book of DANIEL. 45

junction, but also, that this Darius was the son of Astyages, and that the Greeks called him *by another name:* and what this *other name*, given by the Greeks to the son and successor of Astyages was, we learn from Xenophon, who tells us, it was Cyaxares. Nor is it any legitimate objection to such evidence, that the book, in which Cyaxares is mentioned by this polite and learned Athenian, is, on the confession of the exactest judges of composition, a fiction, and not a true history. For granting this, and that it was the design of the author, who was no less a Philosopher than a Soldier, not so much to describe the life of Cyrus, as to make use of such a pretext to convey, with greater address, his own moral and political instructions; still we contend that in a story, then so recent, and of a prince, in whose family he afterwards served, the ground-plot of the whole, and the names and actions of the leading characters, would yet be real. One so judicious as
Xeno-

Xenophon, it can hardly be supposed, would neglect so obvious a rule of decorum: and a great confirmation, that he did actually advert to it, is, that his account is supported by the testimony of Scripture, and leads to a commodious way of removing the apparent inconsistency between the author of the book of Daniel and the profane historians.

II. Having advanced thus far in our defence of the sacred writer, considered as an *Historian*, let us now proceed to examine into his pretensions, considered as a *Prophet*; and try, if we cannot discover as many notes of genuineness, when he takes upon him to foretell future events, as when he professes to relate those which were past. The first, who called in question his prophetical abilities, was Porphyry; a Philosopher of the third century, and famous for his writings against the Christian religion; all of which, by the ill-judged zeal of the Emperor Constantine, were ordered to be suppressed.

He

He maintained, that the book of Daniel could not be compofed by the perfon of that name, who flourifhed in the reigns of Nebuchadnezzar and Cyrus, between five and fix hundred years before Chrift; but was the work of one, who lived almoft four centuries later, about the age of Antiochus Epiphanes; becaufe, as low as that period, the predictions there recorded have in them all the clearnefs and precifion of hiftory; but beyond it, are wrapped up in obfcure and general expreffions, on purpofe, as fhould feem, that they might be adapted to any events, to which a willing expofitor might be defirous of applying them. This opinion, which, at the firft view, appears to be not altogether deftitute of probability, was effectually difproved in a learned commentary, ftill extant, by the celebrated Jerom; who very fagacioufly obferves, that fuch a method of impugning prophecy, from its having been punctually fulfilled, inftead of affording room to doubt or deny its authenticity, is the ſtrongeſt teſtimony of its truth [y]. The next, who laboured in the ſame fruitleſs cauſe with Porphyry, was the noted author of the *Scheme of Literal Prophecy conſidered* [z]: he too, in imitation of his predeceſſor, has collected whatever he could find, to derogate from the merit of Daniel's book, and with much ſeeming complacency has aſſerted, that it was compoſed in the days of the Maccabees. But here again, the miſchief apprehended from a work, deſignedly calculated to diſhonour the religion of Chriſt, was happily the occaſion of exciting two ſtrenuous champions [a], of the ſame name and profeſſion, to engage

---

[y] Cujus impugnatio teſtimonium veritatis eſt. Tanta enim dictorum fides fuit, ut propheta incredulis hominibus non videatur futura dixiſſe, ſed narrâſſe præterita. Hieron. Præf. in Danielem, v. iii. p. 1072. Ed. Benedict.

[z] Collins.

[a] Bp. Chandler: See his Defence and Vindication of his Defence of Chriſtianity. And Sam. Chandler: See his Vindication of the Antiquity and Authority of Daniel's Prophecies.

in its defence: by whom the fraud and sophistry, which deform the whole of this disingenuous performance, were unanswerably confuted and exposed; and on its ruins was erected a firm and solid Vindication of the Jewish prophet; unassailable by all the attacks of succeeding Infidels; and a lasting monument, to perpetuate their own glory and the disgrace of their opponent.

But it becomes us to be more particular in our enquiries into the arguments, by which the genuineness and antiquity of the prophecies of Daniel may be proved. Not that it is to be expected, that we be able to produce an unbroken chain of writers, from whose attestation it may appear, that the prophecies in question, previous to their accomplishment, and soon after their publication, were generally divulged among the Jews; as if nothing less than this were sufficient to shew they were of divine original. Evidence of this sort, where it can be had, is doubtless

less of all the most desireable; but is hardly indulged to us on any matters, that are the subjects of human cognizance; and there are peculiar reasons, why to creatures, in a state of moral probation, it should not be indulged, on the subject of Religion. The truth and authenticity of any ancient writing will then be established on sufficient grounds, if it be supported on evidence, which, though not the strongest possible that may be conceived, is yet, as far as it goes, *real* evidence; if it be not confronted by opposite authorities on the other side; and if at a time, when no testimony of any kind is to be found *for* it, at the same time there be none, that can be brought *against* it. And *such* evidence we certainly have for the book of Daniel.

Allowing then that for the first 200 years after the age, in which the prophet is supposed to have lived, there are not extant any records of contemporary historians, from which the existence either of of Daniel or his predictions may be proved[b]; and it being allowed on the other hand, that neither are there any, from which the contrary can be shewn: there are, who think an authentic document is still remaining, that the book was in high estimation, at least 300 years before Christ, from a singular circumstance recorded by Josephus concerning Alexander; that when that prince was at Jerusalem, the prophecies of Daniel, respecting himself and his conquests over the Persians, were pointed out to him by Jaddus the high-priest. This account, it ought not to be dissembled has by some been rejected as fabulous, as inconsistent with chronology, and as depending solely on the credit of one historian, and him, a Jew. But it ought also to be remembered, there are others, who have

---

[b] "There must have been external evidence concerning the book of Daniel, more than is come down to us." Bp. Butler, Analogy, Part ii. ch. vi.

not scrupled, after a long and accurate examination, to assert its veracity. Let it suffice to mention two, and those equal to a multitude of inferior writers; the illustrious author of the *Connection of the History of the* Old *and* New *Testament,* and the learned Prelate alluded to above: the former of whom has defended the chronological part of this curious incident [c], and the latter has vindicated the historical [d], so as fully to evince there is nothing incredible or improbable in the whole.

At the beginning of the Jewish troubles under Antiochus Epiphanes, and near 200 years before the Christian æra, lived Mattathias, father of the Maccabees: of him we read that, being at the point of death, he encouraged his sons to trust in God, from the many

[c] Prideaux, part i. book vii.
[d] Bp. Chandler in the Vindication of his Defence of Christianity, chap. ii. § i. See also Sam. Chandler's Vindication, &c. of Daniel's prophecies, p. 76—82. And Bp. Newton's Dissertations on the Prophecies, v. ii. p. 16—27.

exam-

examples in Scripture of deliverance afforded to good men, of whom Daniel is expresly named as one; and, in exact conformity to what had been foretold by that prophet, declared to them his own affiance in the divine promises, that the boasted glory of their persecutor should come to nothing[e]. In the same book, where this story is recorded, the author, among other instances of fury committed by Antiochus, relates, that he *set up the abomination of desolation upon the altar*[f]; an expression so peculiar to Daniel, as to be particularly noticed by our Lord[g], and a convincing argument of the general belief of the prophecies at this period.

From the age of Antiochus to that of Christ, there is not the smallest interval, in which a book of this sort could possibly be forged. The Scriptures

[e] 1 Macc. ii. 49—70. Dan. viii. 25. comp. with 1 Macc. ii. 62, 63.
[f] 1 Macc. i. 54. Dan. ix. 27. xi. 31. xii. 11.
[g] Matth. xxiv. 15.

of the Old Testament were now in the hands of several, who regarded them as their dearest treasure, and fled with them to places of security, when it was death not to deliver them up [h]. The calamities suffered by the Jews from their heathen adversaries were no sooner over, than they split into sects and parties among themselves; and as formerly the Jews and Samaritans, from their mutual dissensions in matters of religion, were checks on each other, so as to preserve the purity of the *Law*; so now the disputes between the Pharisees and Sadducees served equally to prevent any interpolation in the writings of the *Prophets:* to which must be added, that about this time, the reading of the Prophets, as well as of the Law, was introduced into the synagogues, on every sabbath day; which alone would contribute to render the corruption of either still more difficult, and less practicable, than it was before.

[h] 1 Macc. i. 56, 57, 58.

The Christian epoch affords the fullest evidence, that the book of Daniel was then reputed an essential part of canonical Scripture: as appears from the phrases of the *Kingdom of God* and *of Heaven,* and the names of *Messiah* and *Son of Man,* all confessedly taken from this author, and none of them first used by our Saviour; although, in compliance with the language of his time, adopted by him, as fitly applicable to himself, and significative of that spiritual kingdom, which he came to establish [i]. Nor ought we here to forget, what has been mentioned once already, and what to Christians is decisive on this point; that the authority of Daniel is solemnly acknowledged by our Lord, and by two of his Apostles; who all either cite or refer to his words, as the sayings of one of those *holy men of old,* who *spake as they were moved by the Holy Ghost* [k].

[i] See Mr. MEDE's Works, b. i. p. 103. *Lond.* 1672.
[k] 2 Pet. i. 21.

SERM. II.

It would be needless to pursue the history of the reception of this prophecy any lower; but from an unwillingness to omit the testimony of Josephus, who published his Antiquities towards the end of the first century after Christ, and with whom this deduction shall be closed. Nothing can be more honourable than the character ascribed to Daniel by this celebrated historian: he repeatedly mentions him as one of the greatest of prophets, who had converse with God, and was eminent for his knowledge of futurity [1]; and he expresses not so much his own sense as that of his nation, at that time and before it, when he asserts that his writings made one of the twenty-two sacred books,

---

[1] Δανιῆλος:—σοφὸς ἀνὴρ καὶ δεινὸς ἐξευρεῖν τὰ ἀμήχανα καὶ μόνῳ τῷ Θεῷ γνώριμα. *Ant. Jud.* l. X. c. xi. § 2. Ἅπαντα—αὐτῷ παραδόξως ὡς ἑνί τινι τῶν μεγίστων εὐτύχηθη προφητῶν· τὰ γὰρ βιβλία, ὅσα δὴ συγγραψάμενος καταλέλοιπεν, ἀναγινώσκεται παρ' ἡμῖν ἔτι καὶ νῦν· καὶ πεπιστεύκαμεν ἐξ αὐτῶν, ὅτι Δανιῆλος ὡμίλει τῷ Θεῷ. § 7.

which

which completed the collection of the Jewish Scriptures [m].

To such evidence nothing can be opposed, unless it should appear from the *internal* structure of the Prophecies themselves, that they were written after the event. And is not the very *clearness*, with which these prophecies are delivered, some may say, and as Porphyry is known to have objected fifteen hundred years ago, a strong presumption, that this was indeed the case? Does not the author of the book of Daniel appear to be too minutely

[m] Εἰσὶ παρ' ἡμῖν—δύο μόνα πρὸς τοῖς εἴκοσι βιβλία· —καὶ τούτων πέντε μέν ἐστι τὰ Μωϋσέως·—ἀπὸ δὲ τῆς Μωϋσέως τελευτῆς μέχρι τῆς Ἀρταξέρξου—ἀρχῆς, οἱ μετὰ Μωϋσῆν προφῆται τὰ κατ' αὐτοὺς πραχθέντα συνέγραψαν ἐν τρισὶ καὶ δέκα βιβλίοις· αἱ δὲ λοιπαὶ τέσσαρες ὕμνους εἰς τὸν Θεὸν περιέχουσιν. *Contra Apion.* l. i. § 8. Josephus does not here relate the names of the Prophets; but his number of thirteen cannot be completed, unless Daniel be reckoned one. And in another place he expressly includes the book of Daniel amongst the sacred writings. Σπουδασάτω τὸ βιβλίον ἀναγνῶναι τὸ Δανιήλου· εὑρήσει δὲ τοῦτο ἐν τοῖς ἱεροῖς γράμμασιν. *Ant. Jud.* l. X. c. x. § 4.

informed

informed of the transactions, supposed to have happened after his death, to sustain the character of a true prophet? With what exactness are the four Empires, with the rise, succession, and discriminations of each, described? The revolutions of the Persian and Macedonian governments are yet more distinctly related: the expedition of Xerxes into Greece; the rapid conquest of that country and of Persia by Alexander; his sudden death, and the extinction of his family; the division of his conquests into four kingdoms; and the fortunes of two of them, Egypt and Syria, from the death of Alexander to the cruelties exercised on the Jews by Antiochus; are delineated with an accuracy, not to be found in the writings of any one professed historian of those times. Here indeed the knowlege of the prophet is at an end; and all that is foretold of a more remote period is purposely involved in terms of darkness and ambiguity. But from the real plainness of one part of his predictions,

predictions, and the affected obscurity of the other, the consequence to be drawn is obvious; that what is related in the former case was nothing more than a narration of events already past, under the pretended name of prophecies; and in the latter, the author was no wiser than other men, nor had any thing to trust to, but the dim and uncertain guidance of conjecture.

This objection is of importance enough to be particularly considered; and the answer to it will form a proper conclusion to all that has been said on the present subject.

1. First then, with regard to the unusual *clearness*, which, it is urged, is discernible in these predictions, we observe, there are many examples of events foretold by other prophets, which are attended with as great and even greater perspicuity, than any of those before us. The character of Nebuchadnezzar, by

Habak-

Habakkuk[n], is as strongly marked, as that of Antiochus Epiphanes, here. Nor is the destruction of Jerusalem by the Chaldæans, or of Babylon by the Medes, recorded by Isaiah and Jeremiah[o] with fewer circumstances of distinction, than the fall of the Persian and Grecian Empires by Daniel. If the person and victories of Alexander, by whom the former of those kingdoms was overturned, are here described by notes and characters, which can be accommodated to none but him; is not the same precision to be met with in what is related of the founder of that kingdom by Isaiah, who mentions him by name, above 100 years before his birth, as the destined deliverer of the people of God from captivity? *Thus saith the Lord, Thy redeemer, I am the Lord, that maketh all things; that saith of* CYRUS, *He is my shepherd, and shall perform all my pleasure; even saying to Jerusalem, Thou shalt be built,*

---

[n] Ch. ii.
[o] Is. xiv. xxi. xxxix. Jer. xxv. li.

built, and to the Temple, Thy foundation shall be laid. For Jacob my servant's sake, and Israel mine elect, I have even called thee by thy name; I have surnamed thee, though thou hast not known me [p]. If it be mentioned by Josephus, as matter of praise to Daniel, that he not only foretold things to come, but also fixed the *time*, when those things were to happen [q]; is not the same punctuality observable in other prophecies; in those, for instance, concerning the sojourning of the seed of Abraham in a strange land [r], the abode of the Israelites in the wilderness [s], and the continuance of the captivity of Judah [t]? In these predictions, as in others that have been already fulfilled, the divine purpose is distinctly ex-

[p] If. xliv. 24. 28. xlv. 4.

[q] Οὐ—τὰ μέλλοντα μόνον προφητεύων διέτελει [Δανιῆλος], καθάπερ καὶ οἱ ἄλλοι προφῆται, ἀλλὰ καὶ καιρὸν ὥριζεν, εἰς ὃν ταῦτα ἀποβήσεται. *Ant. Jud.* l. X. c. xi. § 7.

[r] Gen. xv. 13. Acts vii. 6.
[s] Num. xiv. 33, 34.
[t] Jer. xxv. 11, 12. xxix. 10.

plained,

plained, and we discover with ease the times and seasons, intended by the prophetical expressions: but whatever be said of their perspicuity *now*, it would have puzzled the sagacity even of Porphyry to have discerned the meaning of so much as one, before that meaning had been opened and unfolded in its completion.

2. But it is not so much from the clearness of the prophecies of Daniel, as from their being clear only to a *certain point*, that the infidel is led to conclude they were composed after the event. When Virgil exhibits to Æneas the fates and fortunes of his descendants; when he represents him as raised to an eminence, from whence he might survey at leisure the future glories of his race passing before him in procession, and closes the long line of heroes with the melancholy appearance of the young Marcellus; we needed not the knowlege of his poetical character to have informed us, that the whole of this scenical apparatus was a fiction;

a fiction; as the very distinctness of the prospect as far as the Augustan age, and its not pretending to look forward into any events beyond it, would have convinced us of the pious fraud, had such a fraud been intended. The case of the Prophet and of the Poet seems to be much the same; the views of both are limited within a certain range; nor are we furnished with any marks, which may instruct us to distinguish between Poetical and Prophetical inspiration.

Specious as such a way of declaiming may appear to some, to others, who are better acquainted with the Scriptural, that is, the true, idea of Prophecy, the fallacy will be obvious. For on supposition that *Prophecy came not by the will of men, but holy men of God spake*[u], as they were influenced by the divine Spirit; it follows, that neither the gift, nor the mode or measure, in which it is imparted, do at all depend on the prophet himself, but are entirely regulated by the appointment of Him, who

[u] 2 Pet. i. 21.

communicates the faculty at first, and restrains and guides it in its future operations. Other prophets, as well as Daniel, were sent on particular errands, and for particular purposes; some with clearer, others with more obscure commissions; the predictions of some relating to events near at hand, of others extending to a more distant period: nor can it justly be objected to any one of these ministers of heaven, that their mission extended not to events, which were beyond the natural powers of man to foresee, and which his Inspirer thought not proper to reveal to him by supernatural illumination.

3. Hitherto we have argued on the principles assumed by our objectors; as if the prophecies of Daniel were confined within a narrow compass, and went not lower than the death of Antiochus. It remains that we observe, in the last place, that this concession hath been wholly gratuitous; and that the prophecies in question

question do indeed relate to remoter times; many of which have actually received their completion, and are equally clear and perspicuous with those, which concern the Persian and Macedonian Empires. If the reality of such predictions can indeed be proved, it must be allowed to annihilate at once the whole force of the present objection: and to demonstrate this, shall be the business of the two following Lectures.

SERMON III.

Prophecies of DANIEL concerning the Four Empires.

DANIEL ii. 44.

And in the days of these Kings shall the God of heaven set up a Kingdom, which shall never be destroyed.

THE dispensations of God to man, though various in their kinds, and different in their administration, have all been directed to one regular and consistent purpose; the restoration of the lost posterity of Adam to that immortal life and happiness, which was forfeited by the transgression of their common parent.

To

To announce so gracious a design, and to give testimony to the character and mission of the Adorable Person, entrusted with its execution, was the declared use and intent of Prophecy; which, commencing from the fall, and reaching, through a protracted course of ages, to the general consummation of all things, was calculated to furnish to succeeding generations a suitable, and, in proportion as it was seen to be accomplished, an *increasing*, evidence, that the end and object of *All that God had spoken by the mouth of his holy Prophets, since the world began* [i], was ultimately one, *even Jesus, which delivered us from the wrath to come* [k].

But as the advantages, to be derived from such a prophetic system, could have been but ill secured, had the information, it was meant to communicate, been imparted to *all* nations without distinction; the same goodness, which suggested the

[i] Acts iii. 21.
[k] 1 Thess. i. 10.

end, directed also the means, and contrived that the notices, which God was pleased to reveal of his future dealings with the children of men, should be confined to *one* people; who were selected from the rest, that they might be the depositaries of the sacred oracles, and that in their records the golden chain of Prophecy, let down from heaven to earth, might be preserved entire. Hence it is, that all the predictions in the Old Testament are found, mediately or immediately, to concern the fortunes of the Jews; and that the state and condition of Gentile nations are no otherwise included within the discoveries of the divine prescience, than as they happened to be connected with this favoured family: sometimes employed by the Supreme Ruler as instruments of vengeance, to inflict on a rebellious people the terrible denunciations of his justice; at other times used as ministers of grace, to convey to them, and

to

to mankind, the saving influences of his mercy.

How august and magnificent is this idea of the Almighty's government! Who, when he first *separated the sons of Adam, and divided to the nations their inheritance* [l], did so adjust the clashing interests of contending powers to each other, that all should eventually conspire to promote his own eternal purposes, with respect to his chosen people, and to the religion of his Son. When we contemplate, in the faithful page of history, the multiform and shifting appearances of human things; when *the kingdoms of the world and the glory of them* [m] are passing in review before us, and we see Empires rise and fall at those very points of time, which the great Parent of the Universe, by a fixed and unalterable destiny, had pre-established; when we perceive the mighty power of the Babylonians give place to

[l] Deut. xxxii. 8.
[m] Matth. iv. 8.

that of the Medes and Persians, the Medes and Persians in their turn subdued by the Greeks, and these again overcome by the superior valour of the Romans: we are abashed and mortified by such a survey of the perishing monuments of earthly pride, we feel the force of such awakening proofs of the sovereign dominion of God, and acknowledge, with pious awe, that *The Most High ruleth in the kingdom of men, and giveth it to whomsoever He will* [n]. But when, assisted by the lights which revelation furnishes, we discern these several Empires, under the controul of an Almighty will, carrying on the secret designs of God with respect to his Church and People, and forming as it were a *Prophetical Chronology* to mark the period, in which the kingdom of Christ, for which the world had been ripening for four thousand years, should begin and end; when with the eye of faith we behold Nebuchadnezzar and Cyrus, Alexander

[n] Dan. iv. 32.

ander and the Romans, infenfibly miniftering to thefe fublime intentions of providence, and ignorantly concurring to advance the triumphs of the crofs: our thoughts are relieved and enlarged, amidft the amplitude of fuch conceptions; inferior confiderations pafs away; and no affection remains to the over-whelmed and enraptured mind but that of holy joy and gratitude, in return for fuch exuberant goodnefs, which hath thus amply provided for the prefent and future happinefs of its creature, Man.

Of the truth and juftice of thefe reflexions, what we have now to offer concerning two predictions of the prophet Daniel, contained in the fecond and feventh chapters of his book, and both relating to the fame fubject, will afford a confirmation and an example.

The prophecies I mean are thofe, in which *Four Great Succeffive Empires* are enigmatically delineated; firft, to Nebuchadnezzar, under the form of a *Metallic Image*;

Image; and then again, and with some additions, to Daniel, in a vision of *Wild Beasts*. Not, as has been remarked by the incomparable Joseph Mede, that these Empires were therefore selected by the divine Spirit, because they were greater, either in duration or power, than every other kingdom before or after them; but because each had a peculiar reference to the Jewish state, and in their history might be formed a *Calendar of Times*, which would lead, in a direct and regular progression, from the beginning of the captivity of Judah, to that happy but distant period, when all *the kingdoms of this world* shall *become the kingdoms of our Lord and of his Christ* [c].

But before we attempt to illustrate the completion of these prophecies, it may be of use to lay before you a short account of what is generally contained, and supposed to be principally intended, in the prophecies themselves.

[c] Rev. xi. 15. See Mede's Works, p. 712. 742.

The end and design of both predictions is the same; to exhibit the fortunes of Four Gentile Kingdoms, by whose rise and succession the time, appointed for the establishment of the reign of Jesus, might be ascertained: by which Four Kingdoms, according to the common, and till of late the uncontroverted, opinion both of Jews and Christians, are to be understood, in order, the Babylonian, the Persian, the Grecian, and the Roman. Of the last of these it is foretold, that it should be divided into Ten; and that, from among those Ten, a Power should arise, *diverse from all the rest* [p]; which should *speak great words against the most High*, and *make war with the Saints and prevail against them*, and they should be *given into his hands* [q], for a long season. And this power, so doomed to spring from the ruins of Imperial Rome, is the same, which Protestants contend is else-

[p] Dan. vii. 24.
[q] Dan. vii. 21. 25.

where

where denominated by the name of *the Man of Sin*, and is indicative of that Spiritual Tyranny, exercised by the Roman Church, in its Apostate or Papal state. But besides the description of Four Kingdoms, all raised and supported by human policy and strength; there is a Fifth, mentioned in the conclusion of both the prophecies, to be *set up*, before the series of the former empires should be quite run out, or during the continuance of the last of them, by *the God of Heaven*[r]: which, unlike to every one of the preceding, should *never be destroyed*, but, after *breaking in pieces and consuming all the others*, and among these the persecuting power spoken of above, should *stand for ever*[s]. This character, which, it is obvious, cannot be accommodated to any of the short-lived dominions of this world, is thought to denote the Universal Empire of the Messiah; which certainly began to be erected

[r] Dan. ii. 44.
[s] Ibid.

under the fourth, or Roman, government; and of which, in other places of Scripture as well as this, it is declared, that it shall continue, till time shall be no more.

That this explanation of the prophecies, thus unfolded, is not arbitrarily assumed, but capable of being supported by sober reasoning and true history, I shall now, and with all the brevity that is possible on such a subject, endeavour to shew.

1. And that by the *first* of the Four Kingdoms is meant the *Babylonian*, is plain from the authority of Daniel himself: who, interpreting the meaning of the Image with its Golden Head to Nebuchadnezzar, then on the throne of Babylon, addresses that monarch in these words, Thou, O *King, art this Head of Gold*[r].

2. As little doubt can there be, that the *second* kingdom is the *Persian*, or, as it is sometimes called, the *Medo-Persian:* not

[r] Dan. ii. 37, 38.

only

SERM. III.

only because it is said of Belshazzar, the last king of Babylon, that his kingdom was *divided, and given to the Medes and Persians* [u]; but also, because in another part of this book, where the second and third Empires are again represented under the emblems of a Ram and a He-Goat, the *Ram with two Horns* is declared to signify *the kings of Media and Persia* [w] in conjunction. Profane writers are wont to separate these [x]: nor can it be denied, that the Median kingdom, as *they* understood it, who made it rise from the destruction of the old Assyrian empire, was altogether distinct from the Persian, and began many years before the age of Daniel. But in Scripture, no notice is taken of

[u] Dan. v. 28.
[w] Dan. viii. 20.
[x] Assyrii, principes omnium gentium, potiti sunt; deinde Medi; postea Persæ; deinde Macedones, &c. Vell. Paterc. i. 6.

Medus ademit
Assyrio; Medoque tulit moderamina Perses.
Claud. de Laud. Stilichonis. ver. 163, 164.

this

this intermediate fovereignty of the Medes, till their warring againſt Babylon: and it is certain that, after the taking of that city, it continued only during the ſhort adminiſtration of Darius; of whom it is related, that he governed *according to the laws of the Medes and Perſians* y, and conſequently was King of both; but whoſe reign laſted not above one or two years at moſt; and upon his death, the powers of both nations were united under Cyrus. Hence it appears, that the Median Empire at Babylon, which ſo ſoon expired, is not particularly adverted to, in the times of this prophetic Calendar; and therefore it was not that, but the Perſian, or Medo-Perſian, that was intended here.

3. After the Perſian kingdom, by the confeſſion of all hiſtorians, comes the Macedonian or *Grecian*; begun in the perſon of Alexander, and continued, as we maintain, in that of his Succeſſors, till its final extinction by the Romans.

y Dan. vi. 8. 12. 15.

SERM. III.

This however has by others been disputed; and there are who assert, that the Grecian kingdom not only *began* with Alexander, as all are agreed, but *ended* with him too; and that the princes, who came after him, particularly the families of Seleucus and Ptolemy, who reigned in Syria and Egypt, ought to be regarded as forming a new and separate government of their own. Nor is it of little moment to the right understanding of the prophecies before us, that an opinion, seemingly so unimportant, should be seriously confuted. For mark the consequence: if the kingdoms of Alexander and his Successors both together be considered as *one*; then, because this is clearly the *third* in the prophetical Quaternion, the next in order, or the fourth, must needs be the Roman: if Alexander's kingdom *alone* be the third; that of his Successors will constitute the fourth, and the Roman will be entirely excluded.

Now to the latter affertion, or that which holds that the Empire of the Greeks is not one kingdom, but two, may be oppofed the following objections; which, it is prefumed, to every attentive hearer will appear infuperable.

Firft then, let it be obferved, what is furely of fome weight in the prefent queftion, that the idea, of Alexander and his fucceffors conftituting *two* kingdoms, was utterly unknown to the Pagan writers of antiquity. Thefe all, invariably, fpeak of the Macedonian Empire, whether in the hands of Alexander alone, or parted, after his death, into four fhares, among his principal commanders, as *one*: juft as the Roman empire was confidered by them as one, which was begun by Romulus, and enlarged by future conquerors, defcended from that victorious people [z].

[z] Dionyfius Halic. exprefsly reprefents the Macedonian Empire, from its beginning to its extinction by the Romans, as *one*. Ἡ δὲ Μακεδονικὴ δυναϛεία, τὴν Περσῶν καθελοῦσα ἰσχὺν, μεγέθει μὲν ἀρχῆς ἁπάσας

Secondly,

SERM. III.

Secondly, If the kingdoms, possessed by the four princes who succeeded to Alexander, be esteemed as different from and independent of *his*; no good reason can be assigned, why they should not also be esteemed as different from and independent of *one another:* instead therefore of composing, all together, *one* kingdom, by way of distinction from that of Alexander, as is pretended; they ought, in this way of conceiving of them, to be reckoned as composing *four*.

ὑπερβάλετο τὰς πρὸ αὐτῆς· χρόνον δὲ ἐδὲ αὐτὴ πολὺν ἤνθησεν, ἀλλὰ, μετὰ τὴν Ἀλεξάνδρε τελευτὴν, ἐπὶ τὸ χεῖρον ἤρξατο φέρεσθαι· διασπασθεῖσα γὰρ εἰς πολλὰς ἡγεμόνας εὐθὺς ἀπὸ τῶν διαδόχων, καὶ μετ' ἐκείνες ἄχρι τῆς δευτέρας ἢ τρίτης ἰσχύσασα προελθεῖν γενεᾶς, ἀσθενὴς αὐτὴ δι' ἑαυτῆς ἐγένετο, καὶ τελευτῶσα ὑπὸ Ῥωμαίων ἠφανίσθη. Antiq. Rom. lib. I. Imperium vero Macedonicum, fractis Persarum opibus, in principio, imperii amplitudine omnia quotquot ante fuerant superavit: sed ne ipsum quidem diu floruit, at post Alexandri obitum in pejus cœpit ruere. Statim enim in multos principes à successoribus distractum, et post illos ad secundam usque tertiamve ætatem progressum, ipsum per se debilitatum est, tandemque à Romanis deletum.

Thirdly,

Thirdly, In both the prophecies we are here contemplating, the Four Kingdoms are uniformly represented by as many separate symbols. These, in the vision of Nebuchadnezzar, are four *Metals*, which occupy four different parts of a great Image; in that seen by Daniel, they are four *Wild Beasts:* or, in other words, to every one of the four empires is appropriated; in the former vision, one Metal, and one part of the Image; and in the latter vision, one Wild Beast. Now the Beast, which stands for the third or Grecian empire, is a *Leopard,* having *four Wings and four Heads*[a]: the double pair of *Wings* may be allowed to denote the rapidity, with which the conquests of Alexander, the founder of that kingdom, were completed: but *Heads*, in the language of prophecy, signify *Kings* or *Governments*; and four Heads must mean four Kings or four Governments, into which number the Macedonian Empire

[a] Dan. vii. 6.

was actually divided, after the death of its first monarch. But the Leopard, or third Beast, is made up neither of the Heads alone, nor of the Body alone, but of both jointly: that is, the very integrity of the symbol requires not only the kingdom of Alexander, but that of his Successors also, to be taken in, to constitute one Beast; which is a decisive proof, that in the Prophecies they were supposed to constitute but one Kingdom.

This argument is strengthened by what we read in the 8th chapter of Daniel; where the angel, explaining to the prophet the vision of the Ram and the He-Goat, interprets the latter part of it thus. *The rough* GOAT *is the king of* GRECIA; *and the* GREAT HORN, *that is betwixt his eyes, is the* FIRST KING, *or* Alexander. *Now that being broken,* or the First King being dead; *whereas four* Horns *stood up for it, four Kingdoms shall stand up out of the nation, but not in His power*[b]; or not

[b] Dan. viii. 21, 22.

so powerful, as when the whole command was united under one governour. Here again it is plain, that Alexander and his Succeſſors are both adumbrated by Horns belonging to the *same* Beaſt, or Goat; and therefore in this viſion, as in the foregoing, they are conſidered as Kings that ruled over the *same* Kingdom.

Laſtly, the Hiſtory of the governments of Alexander's ſucceſſors in general, and of the Seleucidæ and Lagidæ in particular, is utterly irreconcileable with the deſcription of the Fourth Kingdom, in the book of Daniel. Of that kingdom it is ſaid, that it ſhould at firſt be ſtronger than the preceding three; that afterwards it ſhould be ſplit into ten parts; and that from among theſe an Eleventh State or Polity ſhould ariſe, whoſe duration ſhould be for many days, even to a period not yet arrived, *the coming of the Son of Man in the clouds of heaven*[c]. None of theſe marks, in any tolerable way of explaining them,

[c] Dan. vii. 13.

them, can be made to fuit the kingdom of the Greeks, either before or after its partition: which, from the demife of its founder at leaft, grew gradually weaker, and in lefs than an hundred years loft great part of what originally belonged to it; which was indeed divided into four kingdoms, and afterwards into two, but never into ten; and far from having any portion ftill fubfifting, was entirely deftroyed many centuries ago, and is now as completely come to an end, as if it had never been.

4. From thefe confiderations we may at length be permitted to conclude, that the *third* or Greek kingdom, from its rife under Alexander, to the time when all that remained of its dominions was loft, by the total defeat of Perfeus king of Macedon, was *one*; and confequently, that the next, which followed it in the prophetical Quaternion, was the *Roman*. And with the Roman the characters, afcribed to the *fourth* kingdom in the Prophecies, exactly agree.

agree. In its first or flourishing state, it was, as it is there represented to be, strong as *iron*; *breaking in pieces* [d] what was left of the Grecian empire, and by that means possessing itself of great part of the Persian, together with some share of the Babylonian. Its second or enfeebled state (which began to be discernible towards the middle of the fourth century after Christ) is emblematized, first by the *feet* of the *Image*, which were *part of iron and part of clay* [e]; and then again, more particularly, by the properties of the *fourth Beast*. But here it is necessary to observe, that by the body of that Beast, no portion of the Greek Empire seated at Constantinople, that is, none of the countries to the *East* of Italy, are to be understood, in the intention of this prophecy; these being already employed in making up the body of the *third Beast*; which is supposed to be still alive, though its power

[d] Dan. ii. 40.
[e] Dan. ii. 41.

be taken away: but under that denomination is included so much only of the Roman territories, as had not been comprehended in any former reckoning; that is, the countries on this side of Greece, or what is called the Latin or *Western* Empire [f]. Now the steps, by which *this* division of the Roman kingdom went to decay, may be distinctly traced. Its first advance to ruin may be said to have been, when it was over-run by the northern nations: its fall was accelerated, when Rome was taken by Alaric the Goth; and it was only not completed, when that Imperial city was conquered a second time by the arms of Genseric the Vandal. A natural effect of the irruption of such barbarians was, that its provinces were dismembered and torn in pieces by degrees; and various Gothic and coexisting governments were erected, which were at last increased to the just number of *ten*. The names of these ten

[f] Sir Is. Newton's Observations on Daniel, Ch. iv. p. 28—32.

kingdoms have been enumerated by writers of the moſt reſpectable authority; and the few variations in their accounts may be readily explained from the confuſion and uncertainty of the times, of which they wrote [g]. It is enough for us, and an illuſtrious verification of the prophecies of holy Scripture, that ſuch a partition was noticed long before by Daniel; and that, among other particularities mentioned by that prophet, as incident to the fourth Beaſt, this, of *Ten Horns* ſpringing all together from its head, was recorded as one; and that theſe Horns were expreſsly interpreted to mean *Ten Kings* or Kingdoms [h].

This expoſition of the Ten Horns, coeval with one another, will facilitate our ſearch into the meaning of another diſtinctive mark of the ſame Beaſt, which is

[g] See the Diſſertations on the Prophecies, by Bp. Newton. Vol. i. p. 460—464
[h] Dan. vii. 24.

signified by the *Little Horn*. They, who contend that the fourth Beast is the Grecian kingdom of the Seleucidæ and Lagidæ, fix on Antiochus Epiphanes for this Little Horn; and would have all that is related in this part of the prediction to prefigure the cruelties exercised by that persecutor on the Jews. But whatever be said of *other* prophecies in the book of Daniel, there are internal proofs that in *this*, which contains the vision of the four Beasts, the person of Antiochus was not in the least concerned, or so much as in the mind of the inspired penman. This Horn is described, as growing up *after* and *among* the Ten Horns, that were on the head of the last Beast[i]; these Ten Horns, we have seen, are the Ten Kingdoms of the Latin or Western empire; among these therefore we are directed, by the spirit of prophecy itself, to look for the Little Horn. But Antiochus Epiphanes was king of Syria; and instead of

[i] Dan. vii. 8. 24.

possessing

possessing any part of the Western empire of Rome, died above 500 years before the division of that empire took place: to suppose therefore he is adumbrated here by the Little Horn, would be incompatible with historic truth. Another and stronger argument is this. Of the power denoted by the Little Horn it is affirmed, that he shall *make war with the saints and prevail against them, until the Ancient of Days shall come, and judgement be given to the saints of the most High, whose kingdom is an everlasting kingdom, and all dominions shall serve and obey him*[k]. These words, we shall see hereafter, are to be understood of the kingdom of the Messiah: but the wars of Antiochus with the Jews *could* last no longer than his life, which was ended at least 160 years before the kingdom of the Messiah was begun: he could not therefore persecute the saints, until *the time came that the saints possessed the kingdom*[l],

[k] Dan. vii. 21, 22. 27.
[l] Dan. vii. 22.

or,

or, as it is otherwife expreffed, until *the coming of the Son of man in the clouds of heaven* [m] : he could not therefore in *this* prophecy be fignified by the Little Horn.

But if the Little Horn be not meant of Antiochus Epiphanes, of whom or of what *is* it meant? And were the queftion to be decided by authority, the anfwer would be eafy; that by this Horn is intended the kingdom of Antichrift. So the Fathers, from the earlieft times, were wont to interpret it: to which interpretation they were led, not only from a careful examination of this prophecy, but from what they had collected befides from a paffage in St. Paul's Epiftles, that Antichrift fhould not be revealed, till the Sovereignty of Imperial Rome were removed. On this account it was that Jerom, who lived when the Empire was drawing to its conclufion, as foon as he heard that the city of Rome was burnt by Alaric, immediately expected the manifeftation of Antichrift,

[m] Dan. vii. 13, 14.

chrift, as then at hand. *He who hindered, says he, is taken out of the way; and we confider not, that Antichrift is approaching* [n]. And in commenting on the 7th chapter of Daniel, he fpeaks of it as the received opinion of all the Church Hiftorians, that this tyrannical, or, as he calls it, this *Satanic*, power was certainly to appear, whenever the Roman kingdom fhould be diffolved. *Therefore*, fays the fame learned Father, *let us affirm, what all ecclefiaftical writers have delivered; that in the confummation of the world, when the Roman Empire is to be deftroyed, there fhall be Ten Kings, who fhall fhare the Roman world between them; and that an Eleventh fhall arife, a* LITTLE KING, *in whom Satan fhall wholly inhabit bodily* [o].

But

[n] Qui tenebat, de medio fit; et non intelligimus Antichriftum appropinquare. Ad Gerontiam, de Monogamia.

[o] Ergo dicamus, quod omnes fcriptores ecclefiaftici tradiderunt, in confummatione mundi, quando regnum deftruendum eft Romanorum, decem futuros reges, qui orbem Romanum inter fe dividant; et undecimum

SERM. III.

But we are not necessitated to have recourse to authority alone, to determine the question asked above; the prophecy itself, attentively considered, may convince us, to whom the character of the *Little Horn* does of right belong. We have seen already, that this Horn was not to arise, till after the Roman Empire had been broken into many independent sovereignties: and it is an undoubted fact, notorious in history, that no sooner had that government, by means of the fierce and free nations of the north, experienced this fatal change, than the Roman Church, taking advantage of such distractions, began to rear its head, and grow up to the full size and stature of the *man of sin*, so graphically depicted in other parts of the sacred writings. Of the same Horn it is said, that he shall be *diverse* from the rest; that he shall have *a mouth speaking great things,*

---

undecimum surrecturum esse REGEM PARVULUM, in quo totus Satanas habitaturus sit corporaliter. Com. in Dan. cap. vii.

things, even *great words against the most High;* and that he shall *make war with the saints, and wear them out, and prevail against them;* but that at length, when the destined period of his reign shall be completed, *the judgement shall sit, and they shall take away his dominion, to consume it and to destroy it for ever* [p]. In which words the features and lineaments of Papal Rome are so exactly described, as *now,* that is, after their meaning has been opened by the event, to be discernible by a common reader. For to what power, in the European or Western world, may we not ask in our turn, can such discriminative notes be applied, but to that Apostate Church; which, under the pretended title of God's Vicegerent upon earth, exerts and maintains an empire over men's minds, not less rigorous and oppressive than that, formerly exercised by ancient Rome over their persons? which, rejecting with scorn the usual homage of earthly princes, proudly

[p] Dan. vii. 23. 20. 25. 21. 25. 26.

arrogates to itself divine names and honours: which, not content with debasing the office of the *only mediator between God and man* [q] by the introduction of unallowed, and therefore, forbidden, intercessors of its own, has authorized, by its principles as well as practices, the most infernal butcheries of his true disciples: and, in a word, in open violation both of the Law and the Gospel, hath filled up the measures of its spiritual tyranny, by polluting the pure and peaceable doctrines of Jesus with the accumulated stains of Idolatry and Persecution.

The explanation here given might be confirmed, by comparing the prophecy of Daniel with what is revealed in the Apocalypse, concerning a similar usurpation in the Christian Church; from whence it would immediately appear, that the *Little Horn* of the legal prophet, and the *Antichrist* of the evangelical, are significative of the same person or power. But such a

[q] 1 Tim. ii. 5.

comparison

comparison will be instituted with greater advantage in another place: in the mean while, from the evidence of Daniel alone thus much may be collected, that Protestants have something more to urge than surmise and conjecture, when they maintain that the corruptions of the Church of Rome are foretold in the inspired writings; and that, with whatever levity or contempt such an opinion may be treated by the dissolute and the gay, there is enough of probability in it to excite the attention of serious men, at least to encourage them to listen to what is hereafter to be advanced, in the prosecution of so momentous a subject.

5. I stay not now to prove, that the *everlasting kingdom*[r], mentioned in the close of both the predictions of Daniel, and ordained to be set up, before the succession of Gentile governments should expire[s], is the kingdom of the Messiah. If what has

[r] Dan. ii. 44. vii. 27.
[s] Dan. ii. 44.

been offered to shew, that the *fourth* of those governments is the Roman, be admitted; the consequence is unavoidable, that the *fifth*, or, as it is denominated, *the Kingdom of Heaven* [t], can be no other than the spiritual empire erected by Jesus. Indeed the description itself, together with the extreme futility, I had almost said the absurdity, of the contrary opinion, supersedes the necessity of formal arguments to justify such an interpretation. One circumstance ought not to be passed by unnoticed; namely, the menaces of certain vengeance to be hereafter inflicted on the enemies of the true religion, intimated by the destruction of the body of the fourth Beast [u]; and subsequent to that, the promise of the universal establishment of the reign of Christ; when *the Stone, cut out of the mountain without hands*, shall *strike* and *break to pieces the Image on its feet*, and become a *great Mountain and fill*

[t] Dan. ii. 44.
[u] Dan. vii. 11.

the whole earth[x]. This part of the prophecies is yet unfulfilled; nor is it for us to ascertain the manner, in which so important a revolution in the religious world will be effected: the use intended by the observation here, is from the symptoms of decline, which are now discernible in the system of Papal power, to point out to you the presumption that arises in favour of the truth of the prophetical denunciations; and from the concussions which have already shook the tottering throne of superstition, to learn to expect, in God's good time, its full and final demolition.

To end therefore as we begun; the two predictions we have now considered, and whose completion may be seen, in part, in the histories of the nations all around us, afford a memorable instance of what was before remarked, that the state and condition of the Empires of this world have all been regulated with a

[x] Dan. ii. 45. 35.

view to one great event, ever prefent in the intentions of providence, the Revelation of Jefus Chrift. Thefe all arifing according to a pre-determined plan, and each at the period, which the fovereign arbiter has appointed, are made, both by their duration and decline, to fubferve the interefts of that Eternal Kingdom, whofe fortunes conftitute the main object of Scriptural prophecy, and which is never to be fucceeded or deftroyed by any other: till the time fhall come, fo magnificently defcribed in our facred oracles, when Chrift fhall have *put down all rule and all authority and power;* and *death, the laft enemy,* being now *fubdued,* the mediatorial œconomy of God fhall be finifhed; and *then fhall the Son deliver up the Kingdom, and be fubject to the Father, who put all things under him; and God fhall be all in all* [y].

[y] 1 Cor. xv. 24. 26. 28.

SERMON IV.

Prophecies of DANIEL concerning Antiochus Epiphanes and Antichrist.

DANIEL xii. 8, 9.

Then said I, O my Lord, What shall be the End of these things? And he said, Go thy way, Daniel; for the words are closed up and sealed, till the time of the End.

BESIDES the Prophecies, in the book of Daniel, concerning the four Empires, in which the Church of God was successively to sojourn, from the time of the Jewish captivity to that of the final establishment of the reign of Jesus;

there are others, in which the history of the *second* and *third* of those kingdoms is resumed; and which, so far as they are connected with the subject of this Lecture, it shall be our present business to explain.

I. In the 2d and 7th chapters, the Persian and Grecian Monarchies were delineated, first by the parts of *Silver* and *Brass* in the Metallic Image, and then by a *Bear* and a *Leopard* in the vision of Wild Beasts. In the 8th and 11th chapters they are again described; first emblematically, and in general, by a *Ram* and a *He-Goat*; and afterwards more clearly, and in the way of narrative, by an heavenly messenger, purposely commissioned to disclose to Daniel, the beloved prophet of God, the things *noted in the Scripture of truth* [z].

That by the *Ram with two Horns*, in the former of these prophecies, is meant the kingdom founded by Cyrus, and composed of the united powers of Media

[z] Dan. x. 21.

and

and Perſia: and that by the *Goat with the notable Horn between his eyes*, with which the Ram was ſmitten and conquered, and which itſelf was afterwards broken, and followed by *four* other Horns that came up in its place; is ſignified the kingdom of the Greeks erected by Alexander, by whom the Perſian empire was routed and ſubdued, and whoſe dominions after his death were ſhared among *four* of his principal captains, and parted into ſo many diſtinct governments: is put beyond the poſſibility of doubt, from the interpretation of this myſterious viſion, made to Daniel by an Angel [a]. The ſame events are recited, and with greater variety of circumſtance, in the latter of theſe predictions: in which the expedition of Xerxes into Greece, the conqueſt of that country by Alexander, its ſubſequent diviſion into four parts, and of thoſe four the fates and fortunes of two, Egypt and Syria (called, from their ſitua-

[a] Dan. viii. 3. 5. 7. 8. 20, 21, 22.

tion with respect to Judæa, the kingdoms of the *South* and *North*), in a regular series from the death of Alexander to the reign of Antiochus Epiphanes, are minutely described [b]. Of this last monarch, infamous for his persecutions of the Jews, the life and actions are recorded at large: his obtaining the government of Syria by flatteries, his expeditions into Egypt, his designs upon that country and upon Ptolemy Philometor its young King, and his being obliged to desist from further hostilities against it and him, by the interposition of the Romans; are all expresly mentioned, or plainly alluded to, in this sacred prophecy. But besides the wars of Antiochus with the Egyptians, the oppressions and cruelties exercised by the same person towards the Jewish nation; his deposing and banishing of Onias, their High Priest; his rage and fury, twice repeated, against the city and inhabitants of Jerusalem, after his return

[b] Chap. xi. 2—21.

from two unsuccesful attempts on the kingdom of the South; together with his profaning of the Temple, and causing the worship of God in that holy place to cease;—these and other particulars are related with an exactness and truth, not to be found in any known Historian of those times [c]. And thus far, in the exposition of both the Prophecies under consideration, all Interpreters, that is, all of name and credit, are universally agreed.

II. After the account given in the 8th chapter of the fourfold partition of the kingdom of Alexander, prefigured, as above, by four Horns on the head of the Goat; it is immediately added, that out of *one* of those four a *Little Horn* should arise, whose marks and properties are enumerated through the remaining part of this prediction [d]. Now that the Little Horn in *this* chapter cannot possibly be the

---

[c] Chap. xi. 21—31. See Prideaux's Connection, &c. Part II. Books the 2d and 3d, *passim*.

[d] Dan. viii. 9—13. 23—27.

same with that before described in chapter the *seventh*, is exceeding plain; not only because the discriminative notes of each are totally unlike, but because they are evidently spoken of as appertaining to different kingdoms; the one, as coming up from among the ten Horns of the fourth Beast, which, we have seen, represented the *Roman* Empire; and the other, as arising out of one of the four Horns of the He-Goat, which, we are told in so many words, exhibited the *Grecian* Empire. There is another distinction between the Little Horns in those two places, which, for its importance, will require to be particularly attended to. In the vision of the Beasts, it has been proved, by that expression was singly denoted the kingdom of Antichrist, and that the person of Antiochus Epiphanes was not in the least concerned: but in the vision before us, though we may perhaps find reason to admit that, in a remote and secondary sense, the kingdom of of Antichrift is to be underſtood, yet, in the obvious and primary meaning of thoſe words, we ſhall, if I miſtake not, have equal reaſon to conclude, that the power predicted by that appellation muſt of neceſſity be reſtrained to Antiochus Epiphanes, and to him only.

And firſt, the *time*, in which this Little Horn was to *ariſe*, and during which it was to *continue*, accords exactly to that of Antiochus, and to no other. It was to *ſpring* from one of the four families, that were to govern the divided power of the Greeks[e]; and ſo Antiochus Epiphanes certainly did; and *in the latter end of their kingdom, when the tranſgreſſors were come to the full*[f]. The latter end of the Greek kingdom was, when Macedonia, from whence that empire began, with the reſt of Greece, was ſubjected to the Romans: and at this period, the tranſgreſſors were indeed come to the full; the legal ſanctuary being profaned,

[e] Dan. viii. 9.   [f] Ver. 23.

and the statue of Jupiter Olympius, denoted here by the *transgression of desolation* [g], being set up by this very Antiochus in the temple at Jerusalem, within less than three months after Perseus king of Macedon had been defeated by Emilius the Consul. The *continuance* of the Little Horn is expressed, not, as in other places of the book of Daniel, by a definite number of *Times* or *Days*, by which words, in the language of prophecy, would have been signified so many years; but by *two thousand three hundred* EVENINGS AND MORNINGS [h]; this singular phrase being undoubtedly chosen to inform us, that in this computation *common* or *natural* days were intended. Two thousand three hundred natural days are Six Years and something more; so long therefore the calamity of the Jews was to last, from the beginning to the end of it: now though we may not be able precisely to say, from what part of the

[g] Dan. viii. 13.   [h] Ver. 13, 14.

history

history of Antiochus the date of these years is to *commence*, yet from the authority of the first book of Maccabees we know, that the sanctuary was cleansed, and the persecution of that monarch was *finished*, about the 10th or 11th year of his reign [i].

Again, the *actions*, ascribed to the Little Horn, are such as may with ease be adapted to the person of the same Antiochus. The cruelty and subtlety of his disposition are well expressed, by his being called *a King of fierce countenance and understanding dark sentences* [k]: his mean and obscure original, by the phrases of the *Little Horn*, and by his *becoming mighty but not by his own power* [l]: and his extended conquests in Egypt and Persia and Judæa, by his *waxing exceeding great towards the South, and towards the East, and towards the pleasant land* [m]. His oppression of the Jewish state in general,

---

[i] 1 Macc. i. 10. iv. 52.
[k] Dan. viii. 23.   [l] Ver. 24.   [m] Ver. 9.

and of the Priests and Levites in particular, are represented, in the usual sublimity of eastern metaphors, by his *waxing great* even to the *host of heaven*, and *stamping upon the Stars*[n]: his abolishing of the Temple worship, by *taking away the daily sacrifice, and casting down the truth to the ground*[o]: and last of all, his sudden and miserable extinction, not by the force of arms, but by a disorder divinely inflicted, and which affected not more his body than his mind, is pointed out in the words, that he should be *broken without hand*[p]. The several circumstances here mentioned agree so well with this noted persecutor of the people of God, and can so ill be accommodated to any other person or power, that I cannot help being persuaded, notwithstanding a great authority on the other side[q], that the

[n] Dan. viii. 10. [o] Ver. 11, 12. [p] Ver. 25.
[q] Sir Isaac Newton: See his Observations on the Prophecies of Daniel, chap. ix. The same interpretation is adopted by Bp. Newton, in his Dissertations on the Prophecies, vol. ii. p. 30—61.

generality both of Jewish and Christian commentators were not *quite* so injudicious as has been asserted, when they maintained, that in the prophecy of the *eighth* chapter of Daniel concerning the Little Horn, Antiochus Epiphanes is the very character described.

If now we turn to the *eleventh* chapter, and compare with the account here given what is further subjoined concerning the same Antiochus, from verses 31st to 36th, as those verses are illustrated by the comment of the learned Grotius; where the several degrees of impiety, successively practised by this abandoned tyrant, together with the exploits of Mattathias, the father of the Maccabees, and of his sons, by whom the worship of God was at length restored, are exhibited in detail; and with which, as I conceive, the prophecy concerning the Kings of the South and North, or of the 3d or Grecian Empire, ends: no further proof will be wanting, that in both predictions the same

same person and events were present to the prophet's eye; and that the difference between the two relations is no more than this; that the character of Antiochus Epiphanes in one is simply narrated by an Angel, and in the other it is unfolded in the way of vision, by the emblem of the Little Horn [r].

Still it is not to be denied, that the *language*, in which the properties of the Little Horn, thus interpreted of Antiochus Epiphanes, are recited, seems to have been purposely so contrived, as to admit of another and higher meaning than the literal. And from a view of this higher meaning, I suppose, it was, that Jerom and the ancient Fathers, at the same time that they expounded the Little

---

[r] It should here be remarked, that Sir Isaac, and after him Bishop, Newton, interpret ver. 31—36 of Chap. xi. of the Romans, and of the state of the primitive Christians after the destruction of Jerusalem; and not, as Grotius explains them, of Antiochus Epiphanes. See Observations on the Prophecies of Daniel, chap. ix. xii. And Dissertations on the Prophecies, vol. ii. p. 132—147.

Horn.

Horn in the *eighth* chapter of Antiochus, were wont to confider that oppreffor himfelf as typical of another and more dangerous power, diftinguifhed by the name of Antichrift. Nor will fuch an idea to thofe, who are acquainted with the dependency between the Jewifh and Chriftian religions, and in confequence of that with the doctrine of Types and Double Senfes, appear abfurd or new; provided there be enough in the contexture of the prophecy itfelf to evince, that fuch double meaning was intended. The fame divine Spirit, which by the prophet Joel had defcribed, in one and the fame prediction, the *near* event of an army of locufts, and the *fubfequent* invafion of a foreign enemy [s]; which had inftructed Ifaiah, at the fame time that he gave to Ahaz a fign of *fpeedy* deliverance from his two adverfaries, the kings of Samaria and Damafcus, to convey to the *houfe of David* the notice of a more *diftant*

---

[s] Joel, Chap. i. and ii.

distant as well as more important deliverance, to be effected by Christ [t]; and which lastly is seen to operate in so conspicuous a manner in the prediction of Jesus, where he comprehends, in the same description and under the same ideas, his first and second coming to Judgment, at the destruction of Jerusalem and at the end of the world [u]; *might* also be the occasion that Daniel, when busied in foretelling the persecution then impending on the *Jewish* Church, should do it, though unknown to himself, in terms, which were ultimately applicable to a yet greater persecution that was to desolate the Church of *Christ*. Such a conversion of the subjects, far from being dishonourable or injurious to the Scriptural idea of prophecy, has by thoughtful men been esteemed as *one* proof of its divinity [w]: and

---

[t] If. vii.

[u] Matth. xxiv. Mark xiii. Luke xxi.

[w] He, who would see the Propriety and Reasonableness of Types and Secondary Prophecies demonstrated at large, ought by all means to consult the

and when, with this double sense upon our minds, we contemplate the prediction of Daniel anew, it is impossible not to feel the most lively impressions of that Antichristian Tyranny, which from small beginnings hath *waxed great,* even to the *host of heaven*[x], and hath *stood up against the Prince of Princes*[y], the Messiah himself, and *cast down the truth to the ground*[z]; and which, from other prophecies as well as this, we are taught to hope, shall finally be *broken without hand*[a], by an extraordinary exertion of divine power. In this mode of interpretation, the Little Horn, wherever it is used, sustains one uniform and consistent character, that of *a Persecutor of the servants of the true God:* in

---

the second Volume of the *Div. Leg.* Book VI. Sect. 6. See also *The Argument of the D. L. fairly stated,* p. 125—143. The same opinion is well supported and explained by Bishop Lowth, in his elegant *Prélections on the Hebrew Poetry.* See *Prælect.* xi. xxxi.

[x] Dan. viii. 10. [y] Ver. 25. [z] Ver. 12.
[a] Ver. 25.

the vision of the four Beasts, it is employed singly to prefigure the spiritual dominion of Papal Rome: in this of the Ram and He-Goat, besides expressing the same notion in a secondary sense, we are to conceive of it as primarily intended to denote the oppressions inflicted on the Jewish church and nation by Antiochus Epiphanes, king of Syria.

III. But however, we may determine concerning the meaning of the vision in the *eighth* chapter, and its double relation to Antiochus and Antichrist; what yet remains to be considered, from the Angelical narrative continued in the *eleventh* chapter, will, when attentively examined, it is hoped, be liable to no uncertainty and doubt. For now the heavenly messenger, having brought down his history of the persecution under Antiochus to the *time of the end* [b], that is, the end of the third or Grecian kingdom, which after this comes no more into account

[b] Dan. xi. 35.

among the Prophetic Tetrarchies; in the 36th and following verses, enters on the description of the fourth or Roman Empire, which by the confession of their own writers began soon after their conquest of Macedon, and whose fortunes from this period are recorded here. *Then*, that is, towards the end of the reign of Antiochus, *a King shall do according to his will, and shall exalt and magnify himself above every God* [e]. By a *King* we are to understand, as in other places of Daniel, a State or *Kingdom*, under whatever *form* it may happen to be administered; and the *particular* Kingdom meant must needs be that, which followed next in order to the Greeks, or, in other words, the Roman. By *exalting and magnifying himself above every God* may possibly be signified the unparalleled success, which attended the Roman arms, or the amazing extent of dominion, to which the Roman nation arrived, from the first reduction of Ma-

[e] Dan. xi. 36.

cedonia to the times of Augustus: to conquer a *nation*, in the phraseology of Scripture, being the same as to conquer the *Gods*, who, in the system of Pagan Theology, were supposed to protect that nation; and the Romans having besides a custom of their own, of evoking the Deities from the cities which they besieged, and inviting them to transfer their patronage from their old retainers to themselves.

In the subsequent words, we have the character of the same kingdom, from the reign of Augustus to the abolishing of Gentilism in the days of Constantine; during which interval, the Redeemer of mankind, called here the *God of Gods*, appeared upon earth, and was not only himself crucified under Pilate, the Roman governour, but his faithful disciples also for a long course of years were barbarously persecuted, till the appointed period of their sufferings was completed. This is expressed thus: *and against the* GOD OF GODS

GODS *he shall speak marvellous things; and shall prosper till the indignation be accomplished; for that, that is determined, shall be done*; or, as the latter words may be rendered, *for the determined time shall be fulfilled* [d].

The next verse contains an account of the Empire, after it had become Christian, and of the corruptions which infinuated themselves but too soon into the new religion. For, not content with forsaking the *Gods of their Fathers*, the Idol-Deities, such as Jupiter and Mars, whom their ancestors had worshiped; a principle of mistaken piety, chiefly fostered by the intemperate zeal of the Emperor Constantine, led them, under the fond pretence of exalting, to debase the purity of Christian Morals: an extraordinary sanctity was annexed to the observance of Celibacy; the laws of ancient Rome, enacted for the encouragement of Marriage, were repealed: connubial love, the

[d] Dan. xi. 36.

SERM. IV.

virtuous source of all the charities which knit man to man, was defamed as impure; and in the end, through the policy of the Roman Pontiff, now openly aspiring to Ecclesiastical Sovereignty, the first law of nature, which God himself *commands to some, leaves free to all*, was impiously interdicted both the Monks and Clergy, *Then he shall not regard the* GODS OF HIS FATHERS: *Neither shall he regard the* DESIRE OF WOMEN; *no, nor any God; but he shall magnify himself above all* [e].

But

[e] Dan. xi. 37. Houbigant, in his note on this verse, ridicules the interpretation of Grotius, qui intelligit, Antiochum non curaturum feminas amabiles; atque in hanc rem allegat cædes, ut hominum, ita et mulierum, ab Antiocho Jerosolymæ factas. On which Houbigant observes, and pertinently enough, perinde quasi non posset Antiochus, mulieres interficiens, unam aliquam aut vero plures reservare, quarum forma ipsi placeret:—Præterea constat, impudicissimum fuisse Antiochum Epiphanem. In the mean time, the exposition of this learned Father himself will hardly escape censure; who, to accommodate the words of Daniel to the same Antiochus, takes away, without any authority, the particle *nec*; and translates the passage thus, *non curabit Deos . . . propter amorem feminarum:* deos sc. *patrum suorum*, quia per mulieres

But there are other and more lamentable inftances of Apoftafy yet behind. For having thus contumeliously violated the natural rights of humanity by unjuft reftrictions upon Marriage, the next ftep, which we are informed this kingdom fhould take, in its proclivity from bad to worfe, fhould be to contaminate the religious homage, appropriated to the one Mediator between God and man, by idolatrous addreffes to fubordinate and unauthorized Interceffors of its own; afcribing to them divine names and titles, invoking them as Champions and Towers of Defenfe againft their enemies, and decorating their fhrines and images with the moft fplendid and coftly ornaments. So it is, that the fpirit of prophecy defcribes this dreadful defection from the

mulieres alienigenas, quas deperibit, avertetur à cultu Deorum fuorum patriorum ad alios Deos. If fuch a licence of altering the facred text be allowed, it will be eafy to derive whatever fenfe we pleafe from any paffage of Scripture.

Faith. *For together with God in his seat, or temple, he shall honour* MAHUZZIMS (that is, Saints and Angels, whom he shall apply to for aid and assistance); *even together with that* GOD, WHOM HIS FATHERS KNEW NOT, *shall he honour them; with gold and with silver and with precious stones and with pleasant things* [f]. The God *whom his Fathers knew not,* in this verse, and the *Foreign* or *Strange* God, in the following one [g], as Mr. Mede with his usual sagacity has remarked [h], is Christ: to the *Jews,* who worshiped the true Jehovah, every foreign or strange God must be a *false* one; but to the *Gentiles,* whose adoration was wholly paid to Idols, a foreign God must of necessity be the *true.* And it is of this true God, or Christ, that we must understand what is further mentioned in the 39th verse; where we are told, that notwithstanding the extraordinary veneration with which

[f] Dan. xi. 38. [g] Ver. 39.
Mede's Works, p. 667—674. 903, 904.

the Roman people should affect to approach him, they should yet defile the honour due unto his name, by dedicating Temples in common to him and to their own false Mediators; whom, in the progress of their superstition, they should appoint as the Tutelary and Local Divinities of particular regions and provinces, and should *cause them to rule over many*, and even *distribute the earth* among them *for a reward*.

The remaining part of the prediction is taken up with relating the punishment, which should befall this Apostate Church, *at the end*[1], or declension, of the Roman Empire; with other circumstances, not yet sufficiently illuminated by the event, and which therefore it will be our wisdom not rashly to presume to interpret. In conclusion is added, as the proper point, to which all the discoveries of the divine will were intended to direct us, and as the completion of God's moral dispensations

[1] Dan. xi. 40.

to mankind, an account of the general Resurrection, and last Judgment: when, the enemies of the truth being now subdued, all *who sleep in the dust of the earth* shall *awake; some to everlasting life,* and some to *shame and everlasting contempt; and they that be wise shall shine as the brightness of the firmament, and they that turn many to righteousness, as the stars for ever and ever* [k]. And with this admonition,

[k] Dan. xii. 2, 3. The expressions here used are much too sublime to have their meaning restrained to a temporal deliverance and a temporal affliction only; and the evident allusion there is to them by our Lord, [Matt. xiii. 43. *Then shall the righteous shine forth as the sun, in the kingdom of their Father:* and John v. 28, 29. *All that are in the grave shall hear his voice and come forth; they that have done good, unto the resurrection of life; and they that have done evil, unto the resurrection of damnation*] is a strong intimation that they ought to be interpreted of the final distribution of rewards and punishments at the last day. Houbigant, as was to be expected, explains them, in his note on the place, of the times of the Machabees: Illi *multi,* qui *dormient in terrâ pulveris,* sunt Judæorum magna multitudo, qui, sævientibus Antiochi præfectis, diffugerunt in locos Judææ & Arabiæ deserto:

tion, thus awfully inforced, Daniel is commanded to *shut up the words, and seal*

sertos et arenosos, & condiderunt se in speluncis:— intelligendi etiam sunt *multi* de illis sceleratis hominibus, qui ab religione defecerant, contulerantque sese ad cultum Græcorum, quos Machabæi, sicubi reperiebant, morte plectebant; ut ipsi etiam cogerentur fugere in speluncas, quia non jam eis præsidio esse poterant Persæ, debellati a Machabæis. Tangi utrosque in vocabulo *multi* liquet ex eo, quod, confecto bello, alii sic recreantur, ut in gloria versentur; alii contra, ut in ignominia. His arguments are two. 1. vocabulum ipsum *multi*, quod de hominum magno numero usurpatur, non de omnibus; nam omnes, non tantum *multi*, resurrecturi sunt. 2. hæc verba, *dormire in terra pulveris*, nusquam reperiuntur, ut significent statum mortuorum. But to these it is answered 1. the word *many* may here be put for *all*, just as it is in the Epistle to the Romans (v. 15. 19.); where St. Paul, speaking of the effects of Adam's transgression, observes, that *through the offence* and the *disobedience of one, Many*, i. e. all, *are dead*, and *Many*, i. e. all, *are made sinners*; and again, that *by the obedience of one, Many*, or, all, *shall be made righteous*. 2. the phrase of *sleeping in the dust* is certainly found to signify the state of the dead, in two passages of the book of Job [vii. 21. and xx. ii.], and may therefore have the same sense here. And 3. although it be true that men in affliction are sometimes represented as *sitting* or *dwelling in the dust*, it

cannot

seal the book, even to the time of the end[1]; and the Angelical narration of *that which is noted in the Scripture of truth*[m] is closed.

IV. The prophecies of Daniel, explained in this and a preceding Lecture, furnish matter for various reflexions; of which the following are none of the least considerable.

First then it appears, that the objection, originally started by Porphyry, and revived by Collins, against the authenticity

cannot with any propriety be affirmed of persons restored from misery to prosperity, that they *awake to everlasting life*. Indeed this learned man himself, when zeal for the interests of his communion does not draw him aside, can use a different language: thus in another place, he speaks of the predictions concerning the Messiah as, many of them, requiring a long series of ages for their completion, and among those, which have not yet received their accomplishment, he expressly includes some of the prophecies of Daniel. See his address to the reader of the Prophets, prefixed to the 4th vol. of his valuable edition of the Hebrew Bible, p. xlix, l, li, lii.

[l] Dan. xii. 4.
[m] Dan. x. 21.

of the book of Daniel, on account of the clearness of its predictions as far as the times of Antiochus Epiphanes, and their obscurity beyond that period, is both irrational and false. For besides that it becomes not us to determine, how far, or with what degrees, whether of light or shade, the author of prophecy ought to communicate the knowledge of futurity; the fact itself, alleged in the objection, is untrue: the several occurrences concerning the Roman Empire, all of which refer to times below the age of Antiochus, being foretold as plainly as those which relate to the Persian or Macedonian Kingdoms, so far as the prophetical intimations are already accomplished: and for the rest, they have no greater ambiguity than any other prediction, yet unfulfilled; of which the completion alone will afford the best and justest interpretation.

Secondly, the opinion of Grotius, and of the Catholic writers, who would explain

plain the whole eleventh chapter of Daniel of the history of Antiochus Epiphanes, and will allow no part of it to have the most distant respect to the affairs of the Romans, is without foundation. For not only the circumstances of Antiochus' life are utterly irreconcileable with such an opinion, of whom it can never with any colour of verisimilitude be affirmed, that he *disregarded* either the *Gods of his Fathers* or the *desire of Women*[n], who is known to have compelled even the Jews to worship the Grecian Idols, and who was infamous for his impure and libidinous disposition; the series of events themselves enumerated here, which reaches from the reign of Cyrus quite down to the consummation of all things, at the day of Judgement, forbids us to admit of so vast a chasm as is interposed between the times of Antiochus and the end of the world; without the smallest notice taken of that great people, which

[n] Dan. xi. 37.

figures in so distinguished a manner among the nations of mankind, with which the interests of God's church and family were and are so intimately connected, and under whose government both Jews and Christians have experienced so many surprizing vicissitudes of prosperous and adverse fortune. A chain of prophecy, so broken and disjointed as this, is incompatible with all our ideas of continuity and integrity, which are in equity to be presumed in a divine revelation; and, in the instance before us, is not more repugnant to sober criticism than it is contrary to historic truth.

Thirdly, from what was formerly observed of the reason, why the four Empires, whose revolutions are recorded in the book of Daniel, were particularly selected to constitute the subject of sacred prophecy, we may discern whence it was, that the life and actions of Antiochus Epiphanes were thought worthy to be so minutely recorded. He it was, who was

SERM. IV.

was fore-ordained to be the instrument of chastisement to the people of God, during the latter times of the Grecian Monarchy; under whom the Jews were to be reduced to the very crisis of their fate, and on the point of being either utterly exterminated, or compelled to *serve other Gods, wood and stone*[o], in direct violation of their law. When therefore this calamity arrived, when this haughty tyrant actually appeared, to defile their altar, and desecrate their sanctuary, and, mad with rage and disappointment, should even dare to meditate the extinction of their name and nation; what else could have been effectual to preserve them from despair, or excite them to a vigorous application to the means of defence and safety, than the seasonable reflection that the same prophet, who had forewarned them of this distress, had been careful also to announce their deliverance from it; that notwithstanding all the tokens of anger and dis-

[o] Deut. xxviii. 36.

pleasure,

pleasure, which were visible on every side, God had not *forgotten to be gracious* [p]; that the *vision of the Evening and Morning* would still be found to be *true* [q]; and that yet a little while, and their Almighty avenger was at hand, and would not tarry? There is another reason, why the destiny of Antiochus should be here insisted on: he, we have seen, was intended to be a figure of him, who has lorded it, now so long, over the flock of Christ, under the denomination of the Pope or Church of Rome: whenever therefore the prophecy should appear to be completed in the type, this would create an assurance that it would hereafter be verified in the antitype; however obscure, and even dark, at the time the prophecy was given, that antitype might be, as well to the apprehensions of the Jews, as to those of the prophet himself. Thus the angel, having revealed to Daniel,

[p] Pf. lxxvii. 9.
[q] Dan. viii. 26.

in the clearest and plainest manner, what was soon to happen in the near event, shews him from far, and as it were in confusion, what was afterwards to take place in the remote one: just as a painter, having expressed in the liveliest and brightest colours the principal and leading parts of his design, throws into shade, or touches in a faint and languid way, the subjects which seem to him but distantly related to it.

Lastly, the exposition of the prophecies of Daniel, which hath now been made, and by the only certain method, that of comparing and sorting them with succeeding events, will greatly facilitate our search into those, which yet remain to be unfolded in the writings of St. Paul and St. John. When Daniel first published his own visions, he plainly confessed he did not comprehend their meaning: his *book was to be shut up and sealed, till the time of the end*; and before they should be at all, or at least fully, understood, *many* were to *run to and fro,* and *knowledge* was to be *encreased*[r]. Accordingly in these latter ages of the world it has happened, that much of the obscurity, complained of in what is here foretold, has been actually removed by the completion: and what to Daniel was represented as a book that was SEALED, by St. John, in allusion, and, as should seem, by way of opposition, to that expression, is called *the* REVELATION, *which God hath shewed unto his servants of things that must shortly come to pass*[s]. Such therefore of the visions of the legal prophet, as have been already fulfilled, may be used as a direction to instruct us in the meaning of, what we are next to attempt to illustrate, the evangelical predictions. And now, under the auspices of such a guide, we may hope to advance securely in our projected work; and to have the pleasure

[r] Dan. xii. 4.
[s] Rev. i. 1.

of those, who, after long travelling in a dreary night, perceive at last the darkness to diminish, and the reddening streaks of the morning betokening to them that the day is at hand.

SERMON V.

Prophecy of St. PAUL concerning the Man of Sin.

2 THESS. ii. 3.

Let no man deceive you by any means: for That Day shall not come, except there come a falling away first, and that Man of Sin be revealed, the Son of Perdition.

WHEN it is objected to the Christian Religion, that, instead of promoting piety and virtue, peace and happiness, among mankind, it has been abused to the purposes of enthusiasm and superstition, and made the instrument of tyranny and persecution to a considerable part of those who have embraced it; we think we oppose a satisfactory answer, when we reply, That the design of the gospel is not yet completed; that we are now but in the midst of a scheme, of whose end no probable conjectures can be formed from the unpromising appearances accompanying its beginning; that nothing has come to pass, respecting either the past or present condition of Christianity, which was not foretold; and that whatever has happened has been of such a nature, as no Impostor could have foreseen, and no Enthusiast would have believed: that therefore the Fact and the Prophecy compared together, far from affording matter of just objection to our holy religion, do indeed conspire to furnish a very considerable argument for its truth; and are admirably calculated to administer repose and comfort to the mind, amidst the calamities and troubles of this disordered state, by teaching us to look forward, with faith and patience,

to

to the scene that lies beyond it; expecting, with humble confidence, the arrival of that blessed time, so magnificently proclaimed in our sacred oracles, when every thing that defileth shall be entirely done away; when the gospel, which has so long been made to *minister unto sin*[t], shall at length bring forth its proper *fruit unto holiness*[u]; and the *earth shall be full of the knowledge of the Lord, as the waters cover the sea*[w].

Now of all the predictions relating to the Christian Church, whether regarding its present humiliation or future triumphs, there is none which more demands our attention, or bears about it less equivocal marks of divinity, than that recorded by St. Paul in his second epistle to the Thessalonians; though perhaps there be none, that has been more obscured by the cloudy imaginations of Interpreters.

I. This has been owing, in great measure, to a common error, that the *Day of*

[t] Gal. ii. 17.
[u] Rom. vi. 22.
[w] Is. xi. 9.

Christ, of which mention is made in the beginning of the chapter from whence the text is taken, is to be understood of his *First Coming*, at the destruction of Jerusalem; and consequently, that the *Man of Sin*, whose character is so minutely described in the following verses, must needs have been *revealed*, before that memorable event was accomplished; whereas, as shall now be shewn, the whole tenor of the Apostle's reasoning leads us to conclude, that he is speaking here of the *Second Coming* of Christ, to judge the world; and therefore *the mystery of Iniquity*[x], which, we are told, was to be laid open, previous to that solemn time, may well be supposed to refer to a remote, and then far distant, period; although it be granted that, in other places of the Apostolic writings, the *Coming* and the *Day of Christ* are sometimes used to denote nothing more than the final demolition of the Jewish polity.

[x] 2 Thess. ii. 7.

First then we are to observe, that the Epistle, of which the text is a part, was principally intended by way of explanation or supplement to what had been written by St. Paul in a former Letter, addressed to the Christians of Thessalonica. In that first Epistle he had laboured to dissuade his new converts from indulging an immoderate grief, on account of their departed friends, from the sure and certain hope of a resurrection to eternal life, of which God had given assurance to them and to all men by the resurrection of Christ. *I would not have you to be ignorant, Brethren, concerning them which are asleep; that ye sorrow not, even as others which have no hope: for if we believe that Jesus died and rose again, even so them also, which sleep in Jesus, will God bring with him* [y]. This state of consummation and bliss, he informs them, was to commence at *the Coming of the Lord* [z]; when

[y] 1 Thess. iv. 13, 14.
[z] Ver. 15.

the dead in Christ shall rise first [a]; and *then* (as if he himself were to be in the number) WE, *which are alive and remain, shall be caught up together with them in the clouds; and so shall we ever be with the Lord* [b]. It should seem that this last expression, in which the Apostle, by an usual figure, speaks of himself as one of those who were to survive the general wreck of nature; added to another remark he had made, that whenever the Day of the Lord should come, it would be silently and suddenly, *as a thief in the night* [c]; had been the innocent cause of the Thessalonians' mistake, as if he had insinuated that the end of the world was then approaching. And to correct this growing error, among other useful precautions, it was, that the provident Apostle thought proper to send them a *second* Epistle: in which he *beseeches* them, by that *Coming of our Lord* [d], of which he

[a] 1 Thess. iv. 16.   [b] Ver. 17.
[c] 1 Thess. v. 2.
[d] 2 Thess. ii. 1.

had

had warned them in his *first*, that they be not soon shaken in mind, or troubled, neither by spirit nor by word nor by LETTER, as if any thing, which he had prophesied or spoken or written, could rightly be expounded to such a sense, as that *the Day of Christ were at hand* [e]. The *Letter* here mentioned alludes to that already sent to the church of the Thessalonians; in which he had treated largely of the resurrection of the dead, and the final judgment. The *Day of Christ* therefore, in this latter Epistle, must be interpreted according to the sense it bears in the former; for it is plain, that in both the Apostle is speaking of the *same* day. But in the former Epistle, we have seen, by that phrase can only be meant the *Second* or last Coming of Christ, to judge the world: therefore in the latter Epistle also, by the same words the same awful period must be understood; and not, as has been pretended, his *First* Coming, at

[e] 2 Thess. ii. 2.

the ruin of the Jewish Temple; which the Thessalonians might have learnt, from the prediction of our Lord himself, was to arrive, before that *generation should pass away*[f], and which was even then at hand, and was actually effected, within few years after the writing of this Epistle.

And here, to note it by the way, may be remarked the fallacy of that opinion, so strenuously asserted by the excellent Grotius, that what is now called the second Epistle to the Thessalonians was written before the first: an opinion, of which it is hard to say, whether it be more contrary to the universal tradition of the Christian Churches, or to the internal evidence arising from the composition; and which nothing, I am persuaded, but a fondness for a favourite project could have induced that able commentator to have advanced.

II. It having thus been proved, that there is no necessity, from the expressions,

[f] Matth. xxiv. 34.

the Day and the Coming of Christ, to confine the revelation of the Man of Sin to the times preceding the judgments of God upon the Jews; let us now consider the character itself, described by the Apostle; which must be owned to be extraordinary in all its parts, and of which the world before had seen neither example nor resemblance. And first we are told, that the manifestation of this *Son of Perdition* should be attended with a remarkable *falling away* [g], or a great Apostasy; the beginnings of which were discernible, when St. Paul wrote his second Epistle to the Thessalonians. What the nature of the Apostasy here mentioned is, does not immediately appear: it may be a civil defection, or it may be a religious one; a refusal of the obedience owing to our earthly governours, or, which is its usual signification in the New Testament, a revolt from the allegiance due to our heavenly Master, which is

[g] 2 Thess. ii. 3.

else-

elsewhere denominated a *departing from the faith* [h]. In order to determine which of the two senses was intended in this place, it will be of use to contemplate the features of this singular personage, which we find delineated, with great exactness, in the following words: *who opposeth and exalteth himself above all that is called God, or that is worshiped; so that he, as God, sitteth in the Temple of God, shewing himself that he is God:—whose coming is after the working of Satan; with all power and signs and lying wonders; and with all deceivableness of unrighteousness, in them that perish* [i]. The power, of which such things are predicated, seems, at first sight, to be altogether different, both in nature and kind, from that of any *temporal* kingdom we are acquainted with, whether of ancient or modern times. Magistrates, it may be said, are in scripture called *Gods* [k]; and the Roman Em-

[h] 1 Tim. iv. 1.
[i] 2 Thess. ii. 4. 9, 10.
[k] Ps. lxxxii. 6. John. x. 35.

perors, in particular, were fond of affecting divine honours, and after their deaths were, some of them, ascribed among the deities of Pagan Rome: so that by *opposing and exalting himself above all*, or every one, *that is called a God, or that is worshiped*, may only be meant, that the Man of Sin should exercise a supereminent jurisdiction over the kings and princes of this world. Allowing this, it must still be acknowleged, that when it is added besides of this monster of iniquity, that he should assume to himself a sovereignty, never before asserted, or so much as thought of, by any earthly monarch, however absolute in other instances; should aspire to rule *as God, in the Temple*, or Church, *of God*; and, in consequence of his usurped occupancy of that holy place, should presume to *shew himself that he is God*; arrogating more than human honours, and claiming to partake of the incommunicable attributes of the Supreme Being, by diabolical pretences to *lying wonders*,

wonders, calculated to impose only on those, *who believe not the truth, but have pleasure in unrighteousness*[1]: these things are utterly incompatible with all our notions of *Secular* dominion, and must be conceived as the undoubted marks of an *Ecclesiastic* tyranny. Hence it follows that, the power in question being thus clearly of the religious kind, the Apostasy, which introduced and is itself supported by that power, must be of the religious kind also; in other words, it must denote a defection from the faith or true religion, and not an unlawful opposition to civil government.

One of the ablest and acutest interpreters of Scripture, whose writings are allowed by all to have been greatly subservient to the cause of revealed religion, has taken much unprofitable pains to prove, that the *Man of Sin* was the Emperor Caligula, who commanded his statue to be placed in the Temple of Jerusalem: but, sensible

[1] 2 Thess. ii. 12.

that Caligula, among the other extravagances of his life, never once ventured to authorize his impieties by miracles, he imagines, to save the credit of his hypothesis, that the Apostle had two persons in his view; Caius Cæsar; distinguished here by the *man of sin* and *the son of perdition* [m], and Simon Magus, entitled *the wicked one, whom the Lord* should *destroy with the spirit of his mouth* [n]. This opinion, like many others maintained by the same person in his commentaries on the Prophets, labours in every part with difficulties that are insuperable. For first, the supposition that two persons are concerned is wholly gratuitous, and without the slenderest support from Scripture, where the account is plainly confined to one character, and to one only. Secondly, it is not true, that Caligula did actually *sit in the Temple of God, shewing himself that he was God*; the command of that Emperor to place his statue there being never put

[m] 2 Thess. ii. 3.   [n] Ver. 8.

in

in execution. Thirdly, there are demonſtrative proofs that the Epiſtle before us was not written till after St. Paul had been at Theſſalonica; which journey by the beſt chronologers is fixed about the tenth year of the reign of Claudius: now Claudius ſucceeded to the empire on the event of Caligula's death; that is, at leaſt ten years before the Apoſtle had viſited the Macedonian Capital: conſequently, to accommodate the prophecy of the Man of Sin to the hiſtory of Caligula, will be to accommodate it to the hiſtory of one, who was dead at the time the prophecy was given. Laſtly, by the Temple in this place cannot be underſtood the Temple at Jeruſalem, unleſs in a figurative and improper ſenſe; in which way it is common enough for the writers of the New Teſtament to deſcribe the affairs of the Chriſtian Church by alluſions taken from Jewiſh ſymbols. Thus the city of Jeruſalem, which was the appointed place of worſhip for the ſervants of of the true God, is sometimes made a type of *Heaven*, or *the Jerusalem which is above* °; and, in pursuance of the same metaphor, the Church of Christ upon earth is represented under the image of an House or Edifice, erected on the *foundation of the Apostles and Prophets, Jesus Christ himself being the chief corner-stone, in whom all the building, fitly framed together, groweth unto an holy Temple in the Lord* ᴾ. According to this interpretation, when it is foretold of the Man of Sin, that he should *sit in the Temple of God*, the meaning must be, that he should erect his empire within the church of Christ: from whence this further characteristic mark is deducible, that the power, prefigured by that appellation, was to be, not merely a *Spiritual*, but, more particularly still, a *Christian*, power.

If the prophecy of the Man of Sin cannot rightly be applied to Caligula, it

---

° Gal. iv. 26. Heb. xii. 22.
ᴾ Ephes. ii. 20, 21.

can with less appearance of probability be adapted to any other of the Pagan Emperors; who, though many of them aspired to divine names and titles, yet none could, in any sense, be said to *sit*, or rule, *in the temple of God*; and whose opposition to the church of Christ consisted not in the delusive arts of pretended miracles, but in an open and cruel persecution of his true disciples.

They who would explain this prediction of the early Hereticks, that infested the primitive Church; or of the rebellious Jews, who revolted from the Roman Government; or of the Jewish Converts, who apostatized from the Christian Faith; are utterly at a loss to reconcile the several parts of the description with the historical facts recorded of the persons, or people, to whom the prophecy is referred. The impious doctrines of Simon Magus and of the Gnostics could with no propriety be called a *Mystery* then to be *revealed*; the witchcrafts of that sorcerer having been sufficiently exposed, when St. Paul himself was yet a persecutor [q]; and the pestilent heresies of his followers partaking rather of the nature of an avowed hostility, which had been immediately and vigorously repelled by the faithful preachers of the word. The opposition made by the Jews to the Roman Empire could not be intended by the *falling away*, mentioned here; that expression, as we have seen, being used to denote a religious, not a civil, defection. And with as little reason can it be thought to belong to the Jewish converts, who, after embracing the gospel, reverted back to Judaism; because the numbers of these were never considerable enough to be stiled by way of eminence *The Apostasy*, nor were they ever united under one head or leader, to whom the names of *the Man of Sin* and *the Son of Perdition* could deservedly be applied. Not to insist, that the opinions hitherto adduced are, all of

[q] Acts viii. 9—25.

them, founded on the common mistake, already confuted, that by the *day of Christ* is to be understood the destruction of Jerusalem.

To proceed with our explication of the sacred text: St. Paul, after enumerating the properties of that antichristian power, which was hereafter to arise, acquaints the Thessalonians, that *the mystery of iniquity* had begun to *work* even then [r]; the corruptions in faith and practice, already generated in the Christian church, being in fact the embryo of that yet unformed and unfinished character, which ere long would be produced into the world, and advance to the just maturity of the Man of Sin. Indeed, as the Apostle observes, his birth might reasonably have been expected at that very period, were it not for a certain *lett* or obstacle, that for the present retarded his coming, and the knowledge of which, he intimates, had been communicated to them before, in

[r] 2 Thess. ii. 7.

his converfations in perfon. *Remember ye not, that when I was yet with you, I told you thefe things? And now ye know, what withholdeth, that he might be revealed in his time. For the myftery of iniquity doth already work: only He, who now letteth, will lett, until he be taken out of the way: and then fhall that wicked be revealed*[1]. From this account it appears, that the *lett* or hindrance, alluded to by St. Paul, was fomething from without, which had then fo great influence and authority, that the tyrannical power here predicted would be unable to make head, till, one way or other, it fhould be removed. The Apoftle feems to ufe an uncommon degree of caution, in forbearing to mention what it was; as if he had fears or fcruples about committing it to writing. And granting the impediment to be, what the ancient Fathers univerfally conceived it, the exiftence of the *Roman Empire*, he had grounds for his fears; as it might feem a fort of treafon againft the majefty

[1] 2 Theff. ii. 5, 6, 7, 8.

of Rome, even to suppose that her Imperial Sovereignty should ever come to an end, or be dispossessed by a power yet more oppressive and rigorous than her own. And it is worthy to be remarked, that the learned Apologist Tertullian, who flourished towards the end of the second century, is at pains to vindicate the Christians from the charge of being ill-affected to the state, and gives it as one reason, among others, why in their public Liturgies they constantly prayed for the safety of the Cæsarean Empire, from the persuasion then generally held, and professedly founded on the authority of this text, that Antichrist could not be revealed, so long as that Empire should continue, and that the greatest calamity, which ever threatened the world, was only delayed by its preservation [t].

[t] Est et alia major necessitas nobis orandi pro Imperatoribus, etiam pro omni statu Imperii,— qui vim maximam, universo orbi imminentem,—Romani Imperii commeatu scimus retardari. Apol. c. 32. See also c. 39. And ad Scap. c. 2.

They

They, who have searched into the times subsequent to those of the Apostles, or to the demolition of the Jewish government, in hopes of finding either an individual person, or an order and succession of persons, in whom the prophecy of St. Paul might appear to be completed, have, some of them, imagined, that the man of sin was Mahomet, the author of the religion still subsisting and called by his name. He, we know, was a confessed Impostor, and took advantage of the corruptions then introduced into Christianity, to obtrude his revelations on mankind; his doctrines, as immoral and sensual as his life, fully justify his being stiled *the wicked one* and *the son of perdition*; and, what is more than all, he found means to establish his religion soon after the declension of the Roman Empire. But however exactly the Man of Sin and Mahomet may seem in some instances to agree, there are other particulars, still more essential, in which the two characters are totally incompatible

ble with each other. The iniquity of the Man of Sin was operating in the times of St. Paul: but Mahometanism was a hasty scheme, suddenly formed and executed by an enterprising adventurer, for the purposes of worldly dominion; nor can any footsteps of it be traced backward to the Apostolic age, or many centuries after it. Of the man of sin it is recorded, that his *coming* should be *after the working of Satan, with signs and lying wonders, and with all deceivableness of unrighteousness*: but the authority of Mahomet was not supported, nor attempted to be supported, by miracles, but by the sword. The man of sin was to be a Christian power: but Mahomet, though he acknowledged the truth of the Nazarite's commission, was utterly averse to the Christian name; and his doctrines are as irreconcileable with those of Jesus, as light with darkness. Lastly, from the predictions of Daniel already explained it has been seen, that Antichrist or the Man

Man of Sin was to be a Roman power; and from what is yet to be explained of the Apocalypse of St. John it will be further seen, that his place of residence was to be the city of Rome: now these are circumstances, which by no subtlety of interpretation can be made to quadrate with the person of Mahomet, and exclude him from any the most distant concern in the prophecy under examination.

It is scarce worth while to mention the sophism of the Catholics, who by the Apostasy here described affect to understand the separation of the Protestants from the church of Rome: because, with whatever art this calumny may have been urged by the writers of that communion, in hopes of fastening on the Reformers the imputation of Schism, by way of retaliation for charging them with the guilt of Idolatry; it is so entirely destitute of truth, that one can hardly conceive it is seriously believed even by themselves: and till it can be proved, that it ever was the

the wont of the Reformed Churches to vindicate their feceffion by Miracles, or fhewn under what common Mafter, fave Chrift, they profefs to be united, it will not be thought, with fober men, to deferve the honour of a confutation.

III. Hitherto we have done no more, than fimply point out, who the Man of Sin *is not*: it will now be expected, that we indicate by certain marks, who he really *is*; meaning by that expreffion, not any *fingle perfon* (for with this idea both the work affigned, and the time required to compleat it, are wholly inconfiftent), but a *fucceffion of men*, poffeffing the fame ftation and character, and actuated by the fame fpirit of antichriftian policy and fraud: juft as, in other places of Scripture, a King reprefents a fucceffion of Kings over the fame nation, a Beaft is ufed for a whole Empire, and the Falfe Prophet in the book of the Revelations, by the confeffion of the Bifhop of Meaux himfelf, ftands for a corrupt communion and fociety,

ciety [u]. Now it is most undeniable, that in the ages following that of the Apostles, a power did actually arise, and within the bosom of the Christian Church, so like to that which is here predicted, that, if it be not the same, it has at least the essential notes of it; nor is any circumstance wanting to an entire resemblance, but the catastrophe or destruction to which the power is doomed; an event, which is yet future, and wrapt up in the venerable gloom in which all unfulfilled prophecies without exception are involved. You will doubtless apprehend, that the power here alluded to can be no other than that now exercised by Him, who fills the chair of St. Peter under the denomination of the Pope or Bishop of Rome. The rudiments of spiritual tyranny, by which this grand deceiver of the Christian world was hereafter to be-

[u] See L'Apocalypse, avec un Explication, par J. B. Bossuet, Eveque de Meaux; and particularly the Notes on Ch. xiii. ver. 11—18.

come

come conspicuous, were laid, even in the Apostolic times; as appeared but too plainly in those dreadful signs of Apostasy, so justly reprehended by St. Paul and St. John; the worshiping of angels[w], observing the Jewish distinctions of days and meats[x], adulterating the word of God with the principles of Gentile philosophy[y], allegorizing the doctrine of the resurrection[z], and denying that Christ was come in the flesh[a]. These errors were not likely to diminish, when, the extraordinary assistances, afforded to the rising church, being now withdrawn, the sacred oracles were committed to the custody and interpretation of fallible men, disposed enough of themselves to extravagate into the baleful excesses of fanaticism and superstition. Accordingly it is a lamentable truth, that no sooner had the per-

---

[w] Coloss. ii. 18.
[x] Coloss. ii. 16. Gal. iv. 10.
[y] Coloss. ii. 8.
[z] 2 Tim. ii. 18.
[a] 1 John iv. 3.

secutions

secutions ceased, and the Empire become Christian under the patronage of Constantine, than a fruitful crop of heresies and rank opinions suddenly sprang up, that choked the heavenly plant which the Father had planted, and were equally prejudicial to the interests of Faith and Virtue. These were chiefly seen in the enthusiastic veneration paid to the memories and tombs of dead saints and martyrs; in pilgrimages to Palestine and the holy city; voluntary poverty, and macerations of the body by fastings and solitude (whence the origin of the Monastic Discipline); the celibacy of priests, and the general idea of the superior purity of a single life. The malignity of such evils from within was not a little encreased by the crafty politics of the Roman Pontiff from without: whose natural pre-eminence of station, as presiding in the Metropolis of the Western world, furnished him with an easy pretext to arbitrate in the many disputes, principally fomented by by himself, among other members of the Episcopal order; an advantage, which he failed not diligently to improve, and which contributed not a little to exalt him to that summit of sacerdotal ambition, to which he afterwards attained, as supreme lawgiver in the Church of Christ. Such in general was the wretched state of things, when the Cæsarean Government, by means of the Gothic depredations, was brought to its end: and the Imperial power, or that which *Letted,* being thus *taken out of the way* [b], the Papal advanced itself in its stead; and perfectly corresponded to the character of the *Man of Sin,* delineated in the sacred writings. The usurped dominion, exercised by this haughty Prelate over the states and princes of his communion, his insolent and illegal claims to depose and murder Kings, and constraining the greatest monarchs to receive their crowns from his hands, are denoted by *opposing and exalting himself*

[b] 2 Thess. ii. 7.

above

above all that is called God, or that is worshiped[c]: his impious pretences to infallibility, and to exercise the prerogative, belonging to God alone, of forgiving and retaining sins, are represented by *sitting as God in the Temple of God, and shewing himself that he is God*[d]: and, lastly, his diabolical artifices to delude a credulous and abandoned world, by the pious frauds of juggling impostors, are prefigured by *coming after the working of Satan, with power and signs and lying wonders, and with all deceivableness of unrighteousness in them that perish*[e].

Thus accurately are the origin and progress of this amazing system of spiritual domination foretold; a system begun in the corruption of all that is good and valuable, whether respecting piety or virtue, and propagated and sustained by the wicked arts of idolatry and oppression. Nothing remains to finish the description,

[c] 2 Thess. ii. 4.
[d] Ver. 4. [e] Ver. 9, 10.

but what is added by St. Paul, namely, the vengeance of offended heaven on this *enemy of all righteousness*ᶠ; *whom the Lord shall consume with the spirit of his mouth, and destroy with the brightness of his coming*ᴳ. This has been in part effected already, by the succesful opposition to the doctrines and practices of Papal Rome, at the times of the Reformation: nor need we doubt but, in God's good time, his gracious promises shall have their full completion; when every adversary of the truth shall be finally subdued, and the Church of Christ, no longer militant but triumphant upon earth, shall once again shine forth in its native purity and splendor.

IV. By way of conclusion we may observe, that from the memorable prediction, whose interpretation has been attempted here, may be derived a clear and decisive proof of the reality of the prophetic spirit

---

ᶠ Acts xiii. 10.
ᴳ 2 Thess. ii. 8.

with which the Apostles were inspired, and, in consequence of that, of the truth of the Christian religion. At the time this prophecy was written by St. Paul, there was not, and had not been, the slenderest vestige of a power resembling that foretold, in any part of the known world; and, judging from appearances only, there was not the least likelihood that any such should arise; much less that it should originate in a Church so averse to worldly grandeur, as that of Christ. Yet that a power of this sort now exists, and has long existed, in the Roman Hierarchy, is a matter of fact, that is not to be disputed; nor can any words convey a juster idea of its nature, than those delivered by the Apostle, so many ages before its arrival. These are things, which cannot be accounted for on any principles of human sagacity or contrivance; and can only be explained on the supposition, that the *holy men,* to whom it was given thus to develope the secrets of futurity, and bring forward its hidden myſteries into day, were inſtinct with ſupernatural communications from the divine Spirit, and *ſpake as they were moved by the Holy Ghoſt* [h].

If the prophets of the New Teſtament were really inſpired, it follows, that the Chriſtian religion is true. For though prophecies unfulfilled may perhaps by ſome be conſidered as doubtful authorities; yet ſuch as have already had their accompliſhment, and can be undeniably proved to have been recorded before the event, and are plainly beyond the reach of human foreſight or conjecture to have invented; theſe ſurely muſt be allowed by every candid and ingenuous mind to adminiſter one of the ſtrongeſt arguments, that can well be deſired, that the religion, in proof of which thoſe prophecies were afforded, is from God; ſince Infinite Wiſdom itſelf cannot be conceived to

[h] 2 Pet. i. 21.

have contrived a more effectual way to authenticate its own declarations; and Infinite Goodness cannot suffer its rational creatures to be thrown into circumstances, where imposture should be permitted to wear such evident marks of truth, and where error could neither be prevented nor cured.

SERMON VI.

Prophecy of St. PAUL concerning the Apoſtaſy of the Latter Times.

1 TIMOTHY iv. 1.

Now the Spirit ſpeaketh expreſsly, that in the Latter Times ſome ſhall depart from the Faith; giving heed to ſeducing ſpirits, and Doctrines of Devils.

THE declared end of the Jewiſh Law being to perpetuate the knowledge of the true God, till the times of the Meſſiah, in the midſt of a world fatally over-run with ſuperſtition and polytheiſm; and the appointed means, by which that end was to be effected, being the

the separation of one people from the rest; it became necessary, in order to secure the beneficial purposes of such a selection, that those, who were the objects of it, should be guarded by the severity of penal laws from the contagion of Idolatry. Yet, whether it were from the inveterate prejudices then generally entertained concerning local and tutelary deities, or from the fondness contracted in the house of bondage for Egyptian manners, or, what was perhaps a more alluring motive than either of the two, the voluptuous and immoral rites of Heathenism; so it was, that, from the very first institution of their Law to the time of their punishment by a seventy-years captivity, this people were for ever revolting from the God of their fathers, and polluting the sanctity of their own religion by the unholy mixture of Pagan impurities.

But we shall conceive a very wrong idea of Jewish Idolatry, if we suppose that

that it confisted in a total rejection of the true Jehovah, as if they denied his being, or doubted of his power: for it appears, as well from the feries of their hiftory, as from the rebukes and exhortations of their prophets, that they ftill looked up to Him as the Creator of the Univerfe, and on all occafions, whether of diftrefs or victory, were ready to own his fovereign right of dominion. But the perverfity, objected to this unhappy people, was this; that they did not confine their religious homage to the God of Ifrael, but contaminated the fervice, due to him alone, with foreign worfhip, adopted from their Gentile neighbours: either adoring other gods *befides* him, as the Hoft of Heaven, or the fouls of dead men, which was the peculiar impiety of their two kings, Ahab and Manafieh[i]; or offering prayers and praifes to their own God, through the medium of *Images*; as in the inftance of the golden calves, at Dan and

[i] Kings xvi. 31, 32, 33.   2 Kings xxi. 5, 6.

Beth-el,

Beth-el, politically erected, to prevent the re-union of the kingdom of Israel with that of Judah, by *Jeroboam the son of Nebat, who made Israel to sin* [k].

Christians, as well as Jews, are under the most solemn obligations, and have the authority of an express command, to acknowledge, as first and principally, *One God, the Father, of whom are all things,* and *to whom* our pious services are to be directed; so also *One Lord, Jesus Christ, by whom are all things,* and *through whom we have access with confidence* to the divine Majesty [l]. And as, during the times of the Mosaic dispensation, none but the High Priest could enter into the Holy of Holies, there to offer incense, and make atonement for the sins of the people, with the *blood of others*; so Jesus, the High Priest of Christians, is the only one, who has *entered into the Holy place, not made*

---

[k] 1 Kings xii. 28, 29. xvi. 26. See D. L. Book V. Sect. 2.

[l] 1 Cor. viii. 6. Ephes. ii. 18. iii. 12.

with

with hands, with power to *appear in the presence of God*, there to offer the spiritual incense, which is *the prayers of the Saints* [m], after having, *with his own blood, obtained eternal redemption for us* [n]. Yet, whether through an affectation of *humility*, and a fear of approaching too nigh to God; or through a mistaken apprehension that they were not *compleat* [o] in Christ, but had need of other patrons and helpers besides him; there have been Christians, who have made to themselves *gods many and lords many* [p]; *not holding the head, from which all the body* hath effectual *nourishment* supplied [q]; and transferring the honour, appropriated to Christ alone, to Angels and to Saints; whom they have vainly addressed as the givers of spiritual grace and comfort, and whose power they have invoked in all the forms and language of devotion.

[m] Rev. v. 8.
[n] Heb. ix. 11, 12. 24, 25.
[o] Coloss. ii. 18. 10.
[p] 1 Cor. viii. 5.   [q] Coloss. ii. 19.

But

But here again we shall do well to observe, that as the Israelites, even in their most corrupt state, never wholly withdrew their allegiance from the true God, but only worshiped Him together with the false gods of the nations round about them, or under the representation of Calves and Images; so Christians, who are charged with thus detracting from the merits of Christ, are not supposed to have incurred so great a guilt, by a total renunciation of his religion; but by setting up other Intercessors besides, and in conjunction with, Him: in direct repugnance to that precept of scripture, which teaches, that as *there is but one God,* so there is also but *one Mediator between God and man*[r]; whose incommunicable prerogative it is, to receive and present the requests and thankfgivings of pious persons to His Father and Our Father, and who *is able to save to the uttermost them that*

[r] 1 Tim. ii. 5.

come unto God by Him, seeing He ever liveth to make intercession for us [s].

Hence it follows, that as the perfection of Jewish Worship consisted in having none other Gods but one, and the essence of Jewish Idolatry in acknowledging a plurality; so the perfection of Christian Worship consists in having none other Mediator but Christ, and the essence of what may fitly be called Christian Idolatry in owning other Mediators besides him. And as the Jews were guilty of violating the law of Moses, not only when they prayed to a multitude of gods, but also when they prayed to the true God under any sensible likeness or symbol; so Christians offend against the law of Christ, not only when they have recourse to other Mediators, but also when they offer their supplications to Him, by an image or visible representation.

This account of the nature of Jewish and Christian Worship and Idolatry will open

[s] Heb. vii. 25.

open the way to the elucidation of what is now to engage our attention, the prophecy, recorded in the text; in which St. Paul, predicting, as in a former Epistle, that great defection of the Christian world, which was to happen in the *latter times*, foretells that it should be accompanied, as with other superstitious observances, such as *forbidding to marry*, and *commanding to abstain from meats* (both which had begun to insinuate themselves even in the Apostolic age), so chiefly with the revival of the ancient and exploded worship of *Demons*; expressed here by *giving heed to seducing spirits and doctrines of Devils*[t]. But besides this characteristic mark, by which so solemn a revolt should be discriminated from all others, two other notes of distinction are also subjoined; one, that it should be that very *departing from the faith*, of which the Church had been already forewarned by an express revelation from the divine Spirit;

[t] 1 Tim. iv. 1. 3.

Spirit; the other, that its arrival was not to be expected till the *latter times*.

In enlarging on each of these particulars, and in the order they have now been mentioned, we shall be furnished, as we go along, with the most undoubted proofs of the completion of this prophecy in the Apostasy of Papal Rome; from whence will appear the truth and justice of that accusation, so frequently insisted on by Protestants, when they impugn the established worship of that communion, as Idolatrous and Antichristian.

I. First then let it be remarked, that it was a confessed principle of Pagan Theology, that the Sovereign of the Universe was of too sublime a nature to humble himself to behold what was going forward in so obscure and sordid a corner as this earth; as well as too pure to be immediately approached by a creature, degraded to so low a rank in the scale of beings as Man. The care and government of the world, it was believed, was delegated to the

the vicegerency of inferior agents, better known by the name of DEMONS; a sort of demi-gods, or subaltern divinities, by whose ministry the whole intercourse between gods and men, such as the reciprocation of prayers and benefits, petitions and supplies, was managed and carried on. It were easy to support the position here advanced by a tedious heap of quotations, from the writings of the Platonists (which to bring together would be but to abuse your patience [u]): it is of more importance to observe, that the Demons, into whose original we are now enquiring, were of two kinds; one, of a higher order, who had never been imprisoned or linkt with a human body, such as *Angels* are conceived by us; the other, of an inferior class, the souls of departed heroes, who, during their abode on earth, had been the Founders and Benefactors of human society, and were now exalted to heaven,

[u] See the very learned Treatise of Mr. Mede, of the *Apostasy of the Latter Times*; particularly ch. 3—7. See also D. L. B. III. Sect. 4.

and canonized after the manner of Romish Saints. Of these Demons it was that the Athenians, who of all the Greeks were most addicted to the custom of adopting foreign gods, imagined St. Paul to speak, when he *preached to them Jesus, and* his *resurrection* [w] from the dead: and to the same idol-deities there is an allusion in the first Epistle to the Corinthians; where it is said, that *the things which the Gentiles sacrificed, they sacrificed to Demons, not to God*; and that Christians could not *partake*, at one and the same time, *of the table and cup of the Lord*, and of *the table and cup of Demons* [x]. When therefore we find the great Apostle of the Gentiles, whose extensive learning must have introduced him to the most intimate acquaintance with the religious rites of Paganism, expressly declaring, that the Apostasy of the latter times should be principally distinguished by *giving heed to doctrines con-*

---

[w] Acts xvii. 18. See D. L. B. II. Sect. 6.
[x] 1 Cor. x. 20, 21.

cerning

cerning Demons (for so the words had better have been translated), of whose office we have seen it was, to mediate and intercede between the gods and mortals; and then compare with this prediction the avowed principles of the Church of Rome, according to which Angels and Saints are both invoked under the same character of mediators and intercessors, *without*, and therefore *against*, the authority, expressed or implied, of God's word; so entire a conformity in the *thing* annihilates any trifling difference in the *name*, and from the perfect likeness in the copy we are forbid to hesitate in pronouncing about the original.

But it is not only in the *objects* of worship, that this similitude between the Demonology of the Gentiles and that of modern Rome is discernible, but also in the *mode* in which such worship is performed. The Pagan adoration of Demons was externally paid to material Images and Columns, animated, as was supposed, by an intelligence, communicated by the god in whose honour they were erected, and there confined, as within a sacred inclosure, from whence there was no escape. And the same respect was shewn to the Remains and Sepulchres of Demons, as to their Statues and Pillars. Now who sees not, that to these ceremonies, the customs prescribed and practised among the votaries of Papal Rome, such as the prostrations made to Images, to the Cross, and at the elevation of the Host, together with the superstitious regard to the Relics and Tombs of Martyrs, exactly correspond? In vain the advocates of that corrupted church endeavour to elude the crime of Idolatry, so justly charged upon them on account of such observances, by pleading here, that these outward memorials are only honoured with a *relative* worship; that it is not the substance or matter, of which they are composed, but the persons, of whom they bear the impression, or suggest the remembrance,

brance, to which their reverential regards are really paid: becaufe, with whatever plaufibility, or even *truth*, this argument may be urged, as to the wifer and more informed part of that communion, the vulgar worfhipers, we affirm, will never make, or will never retain, any fuch diftinction; the adoration, which is directed by them to a fenfible object, will terminate in that object, and look no farther; and the fign or fymbol, which was employed at firft as the *means* of devotion, will foon be refted and confided in, as an *end*. The Jews were forbidden, in the moft folemn manner, to make any fimilitude of God, under any form: and if the Angel, who appeared to St. John, rejected the homage of that Apoftle offered to himfelf, when prefent, and in perfon, in terms of abhorrence;—*See thou do it not*; *I am thy fellow-fervant*; *worfhip God*[y];—the fame homage, paid to his reprefentation, when abfent, it may be pre-

[y] Rev. xxii. 8, 9.

sumed, would have been still more displeasing. No command, or even permission, concerning the praying to Images, whether meant as memorials of Christ or of his Saints, is so much as pretended to be found in scripture: and in the following words of Moses, which, though originally spoken with respect to the Supreme Being, are not without their force, when applied to any other object of worship, may be discovered no slight tokens of a divine prohibition: *Take good heed unto yourselves, for ye saw no similitude, on the day that the Lord spake to you in Horeb, out of the midst of the fire; lest ye corrupt yourselves, and make the similitude of any figure; lest ye forget the covenant of the Lord your God, and make you a graven image, or the likeness of any thing which the Lord thy God hath forbidden thee: for the Lord thy God is a consuming fire, even a jealous God*[z].

[z] Deut. iv. 15, 16. 23, 24.

Whether the conformity between Pagan and Popish Worship, which has been here insisted on, were owing to direct *imitation*, or arose from the natural workings of superstition, which in similar situations produces similar effects, has been matter of dispute[a]. They, who contend that the religion of Christian Rome is immediately derived from that of the heathen city, have, it must be allowed, alleged a variety of instances, in which the rites and ceremonies are the same in both: but it must also be acknowledged, that from this circumstance alone no decisive proof can be drawn, that one was formed on the plan, and modelled after the pattern, of the other; because there are several examples of conformity to be found among nations, between whom, we are sure, there never was the smallest intercourse or communication, where

---

[a] See the Letter from Rome, by Dr. Middleton; and the Remarks on that Letter by Bp. Warburton, D. L. Book IV. Sect 6. at the end.

therefore there cannot be the shadow of a reason to assert, that their common customs were traductive from each other. Many of the gods of the ancient Gauls and Suevi, and those of the later Greeks and Romans, have been remarked to differ only in name; whence some writers, misled by this resemblance, have positively declared for their identity: yet more learned and accurate investigators of antiquity have fully exposed the fallacy of this opinion; which had never any other support than on the attributes, ascribed to the divinities of those several countries; which attributes, on account of the rise of the gods themselves from humanity, were, and could not but be, the same [b]. A like correspondency has been observed by a fine critic between the manners of the fabulous Greeks, as delineated in the well-known poems of Homer, and those of the Feudal Barons, as represented in the works of the Gothic

[b] See D. L. Book IV. Sect. 5.

romancers [c]: yet he, who should say that the latter of these were copied from the former, would undoubtedly fall into a gross mistake; since the agreement between them may so naturally be accounted for, from the similarity of the political states of Greece and Europe, at the two periods described, which gave an unity of character to both, though at the same time both were equally originals. But, not to dwell any longer on a controversy, which after all is not of the most important kind; let it be remembered, that which ever way this dispute be determined, the *fact* itself, of the actual revival of the Gentile Demonology in the Church of Christ, stands clear of any objections that may be brought against either hypothesis: and the fact is all, that a believer, or an interpreter, of prophecy need be concerned for.

II. The second mark, by which the defection of Christians is described in the

[c] See the Letters on Chivalry and Romance; Letter iv.

text, is this; that it was to be the same *departing from the faith*, of which *the Spirit* had *expressly spoken* before; where by *expressly* can only be meant, that it had been mentioned in express words. Now it is certain that St. Paul was himself enabled, by a supernatural revelation, to foretell the *falling away*, of which he forewarns his son Timothy here, when he wrote his second Epistle to the Thessalonians [d]: and there are who think, it is that Epistle, to which he alludes in this place. But a better opinion is, that the prediction meant is that contained in the eleventh chapter of the book of Daniel, and explained in a former Lecture; where the corruptions of the Christian Church, which were hereafter to be occasioned by the Roman Hierarchy, are made to consist in the same unnatural union of the worship of Demons, or tutelary gods, with that of Christ, accompanied too with the same prohibition of

[d] 2 Thess. ii. 3.

mar-

marriage, as is recorded in this Epistle[e]: so that the substance as well as subject of both descriptions being alike, it is most probable, that the discoveries of the Jewish prophet were those referred to by the Christian Apostle.

III. This conjecture will be confirmed by adverting to the *period*, within which the Apostasy foretold was to take place; which, it is said, should be *in the latter times*. By the *latter times* are signified, in the ordinary acceptation of the phrase, the times subsequent to the establishment of Christianity, as the *former times* are those which preceded that great æra. But there is another division of time, made use of in scripture, which is founded on the succession of the Four Empires, whose fortunes are related at large by Daniel; during the *last* of which, the kingdom of Christ was to be erected, and to *stand for ever*[f]. With reference to this division, the *last times*, when spoken

[e] Dan. xi. 36—40.
[f] Dan. ii. 44.

of in general, are the times of the laſt, that is, the Roman, kingdom; and the *latter times*, in particular, are the latter times of the ſame kingdom. Now Daniel, we have ſeen, in the prophecy in queſtion, expreſsly limits the appearance of Antichriſt, denoted by the *Little Horn*, to the preciſe period, when the fourth or Roman Empire ſhould be diſmembered, and broken into *ten* parts; among which ten this new power was gradually to ſpring up, and *make war with the ſaints, and prevail againſt them*, until *his dominion* were finally *taken away* [g]. By the *latter times* therefore, according to this notation, are to be underſtood the times of the reign of Antichriſt, or the *Little Horn:* and, St. Paul having a retroſpect, in other parts of the prediction, to what had been before revealed, concerning the ſame events, to Daniel; it is of *theſe* times we muſt ſuppoſe him to ſpeak, when he ſays *the ſpirit had ſpoken expreſsly* that in them men

[g] Dan. vii. 8. 21. 26.

ſhould

should *depart*, or apostatize, *from the* Christian *faith*.

IV. To collect then the several scattered observations on this prophecy into one view. The Apostasy, here described, is not only expressed, in general, by the phrases, *departing from the faith*, and *giving heed to seducing spirits*, or erroneous doctrines; but those doctrines themselves are particularly specified, of which the chief and principal is declared to be the Worship of Demons, which is Idolatry. It is this, that constitutes the essence of that amazing corruption, which as a cloud was to overspread the face of the Christian Church, and by which it is stigmatized and distinguished from the blasphemies and heretical opinions of every other age, before and after it. But besides the kind and quality of the doctrines taught, we are directed, for further certainty, to an ancient prediction of the Old Testament, in which the same religious defection is recorded, and in the most direct and positive

sitive terms, by the Holy Spirit: and, that no proof might be wanting, the Time, in which this revolt was to happen and be succesful, is defined by a form of speech, whose meaning had been already settled and ascertained by the authority of Daniel. Let any one now, after seriously reflecting on these prophetic characters, be pleased but to set over against them the corresponding facts, as realized in the history of the now-existing tyranny of Papal Rome; in which Demon-Worship, or the invocation of false Mediators, and the superstitious use of Images in the solemnities of divine adoration, are authoritatively enjoined and practised: let him add too, that these corruptions, together with others of an inferior sort, were actually introduced at the very time, when the Western Empire, with its Imperial Head, was destroyed, and the Roman Pontiff erected himself on its ruins; and that this circumstance also had been expressly noticed, long before, by one of the

the most renowned of the Jewish Prophets: and without taking in, what yet is necessary to give the argument its *full* force, the concurring evidence arising from other prophecies, the wonderful appearances of completion to be found in this, must, I think, be allowed to be of great and considerable weight; of much too great, to be carelessly treated as nothing, or to be resolved at once into one of those numerous coincidencies, which time and chance are ever producing in the ceaseless revolution of human things.

But as in the most forlorn and helpless state of natural religion, God never *left himself without witness* [h], but afforded sufficient proofs, by which the discerning few might be abundantly convinced of his power and goodness; so in the worst and most calamitous condition of his revealed will, the same Almighty Being, always watchful for the happiness of his rational creatures, has never suffered vice

[h] Acts xiv. 17.

and

and error so far to prevail, but that there have yet been some *burning and shining lights* [i], which have prevented the darkness from becoming total, or the glorious lamp of the gospel from being quite extinguished. And as in the days of Ahab, Elijah, when complaining of the Apostasy of the Israelites, and ready to suppose that he *only remained of the prophets of God, and that they sought his life to take it away,* received for answer, that there were then *left seven thousand men,* untainted with the general idolatry, and *who had never bowed the knee to Baal* [k]; even so in these *latter times,* there has always been *a remnant* [l], who have stedfastly adhered to the true principles of the Christian religion, and whom no temptations, whether of prosperity or persecution, have been able to seduce from their promised allegiance to Christ. This is

[i] John v. 35.
[k] Kings xix. 10. 14. 18.
[l] Rom. xi. 2—6.

not obscurely intimated in the text, when it is said that SOME should *depart from the faith*; where though *some*, according to its usual signification in Scripture, undoubtedly means the greater part, yet it also implies an exception, with regard to a few, who should still retain their integrity, notwithstanding the prevailing errors. Amongst this *some* it is our lot, through the goodness of an over-ruling providence, to be cast; and in the midst of all that Antichristian Idolatry, with which other countries are overwhelmed, to be selected, like another chosen people, to live in a land, where the gospel of Christ is professed in its native purity. It becomes us to manifest the sense we have of so invaluable a blessing, by *walking worthy* of the *high calling, wherewith we are called* [m], and by transferring the Reformation, thus happily effected in our Religion, to our lives; that *building up our-*

---

[m] Ephes. iv. 1. Philipp. iii. 14.

selves

selves in our most holy Faith [n], and *adorning the doctrine of God our Saviour* [o] by a holy conversation, we may never be suffered to *fall from our own stedfastness*, but *grow in grace and in the knowledge of our Lord Jesus Christ* [p].

[n] Jude 20.
[o] Titus ii. 10.
[p] 2 Pet. iii. 17, 18.

SERMON VII.

The Authority of the Apocalypse, and the Time when it was written.

REV. i. 3.

Blessed is he that readeth, and they that hear, the words of this prophecy, and keep those things which are written therein; for the time is at hand.

THE predictions concerning the rise and fall of Antichrist, so far as these are to be found in the book of Daniel and the Epistles of St. Paul, having been already considered in the preceding Lectures; it now remains that,

accord-

SERM. VII.

according to our proposed plan, we proceed to others yet more important, which are recorded, for the consolation of the faithful, in the Revelation of St. John.

On the most cursory view of this prophecy it is obvious, that, as well on account of its matter and method, as of the symbolical character that pervades the whole, it is of a much more mysterious and dark complexion than any other, either of the Old or New Testament. Indeed so mysterious and so dark, that, as modern sceptics would have us believe, we can never hope to see any clear and consistent system deduced from it: for a proof of which we are referred to the various schemes of interpretation, invented by Christians of opposite communions, all of whom have been fond to find their own cause and fortunes foretold in it; whose discordant opinions are therefore by the wiser few to be regarded as nothing better than the whimsies of a warm or distempered imagination; visionary and illusive,

illusive, like the figures seen in the clouds, which appear under different forms, according to the fancy and disposition of the beholder.

But to repress the libertinism of such scorners, or yet to expose the indiscretions of former interpreters, is none of our concern. Our business, with respect to this extraordinary book, is of a more interesting kind; to lay before you the evidences of its authority, to point out the way in which the obscurity, peculiar to it, may be removed, to unfold its general scope and design, and lastly to examine whether, and how far, the event has corresponded to the whole, or any part, of the prediction. And to sober and serious inquirers, to those who to a coolness and severity of judgment, capable of penetrating the reasons of this singular species of composition, have added, what is a yet more essential qualification in a reader of God's word, a sincere and teachable and humble mind, such a mode of investigation may, it is hoped, administer some degree of satisfaction. For these are the persons to whom, it must be supposed, the promised *blessing* in the text is principally addressed; whose characters are emphatically described by our Lord, when, rapt in the contemplation of the counsels of providence in offering the gospel to the poor, he thus expresses his own acknowledgment of the wisdom as well as goodness of such a procedure: *I thank thee, O Father, Lord of heaven and earth, because thou hast hid these things from the wise and prudent, and hast revealed them unto babes. Even so, Father! for so it seemed good in thy sight* q.

I. First then, as it will be in vain to busy ourselves about the manner of interpreting this prophetical book, unless we be previously convinced that it is the genuine production of him, whose name it bears; it will be necessary, before we proceed to any other inquiry, to bring

q Math. xi. 25, 26.

together the arguments which have been advanced, and which seem to be conclusive, in favour of its authenticity.

1. Now here it is a remarkable circumstance, and what perhaps distinguishes the Apocalypse from every other portion of the New Testament, that it was universally received, as the work of John the Evangelist, by those who lived nearest the times of its publication, without a single person appearing to question its authority. The *date* of this book, which, as we shall see hereafter, does not commence till near the end of the first century after Christ, sufficiently accounts for the silence of the earliest of the Fathers concerning it. Two of the most illustrious, among those who first mention it, are Justin the Martyr, converted to the faith within thirty years after it was written, and Irenæus, the constant hearer of Polycarp, who was himself a disciple of St. John. Both agree in positively ascribing the Apocalypse to this Apostle; and the latter

latter in particular was curious to search into all the approved copies, in order to satisfy himself concerning a dubious passage, the true reading of which, he relates, was also confirmed to him by those, *who knew the author face to face*. Other testimonies may be added from Clemens of Alexandria, the Latin Father Tertullian, and the famous Origen; all living within 120 years from the death of the Evangelist; and by whom, though situated in different and distant regions, the book was uniformly numbered among the Apostolic writings, without the smallest doubt and hesitation.

Nor let it be urged, as of weight to enervate the evidence of these venerable men, that some, or perhaps all, were known to adopt opinions on other points, allowed to be false or frivolous [r]. For

---

[r] See a thing called Dictionnaire Philosophique Portatif, Art. *Apocalypse*; where this objection is set off with all the false colourings that the most disingenuous of writers could lay upon it.

however this objection may affect such of their assertions as relate to matters of speculation, where the sincerity of those who embrace them is indeed no proof of their truth; it can have no influence in weakening their attestations to a matter of fact, concerning which they had every opportunity of informing themselves, and which they concur to affirm, with all the marks of artlessness and simplicity.

2. Such was the state of credit in which the Apocalypse was generally held, during the two first ages of the Christian Church; when at the beginning of the third, or towards the end of the preceding century, its canonical authority began to be doubted, and on the following occasion. An opinion was propagated at Rome, by one Proculus, a Montanist, and founded, as should seem, on what had formerly been taught by the heretic Cerinthus, concerning the reign of Christ with the saints on earth; the whole period of which, as that impostor

had laboured to inculcate, was to be employed in nuptial entertainments and carnal indulgences. Many other notions were espoused by the same Cerinthus, utterly repugnant to the doctrines of the Apocalypse; and even his ideas of the Millennium, it might easily have been shewn, were not those of this sacred book. However as Proculus, to support his favourite delusion, had availed himself of the prophecies recorded there; Caius, a Presbyter of Rome, as the most effectual method of silencing his adversary at once, took upon him to controvert the genuineness of the book itself[a]; the writer of which, he maintained, was no other than Cerinthus, who was certainly contemporary with St. John, and who had artfully assumed the name of that Apostle, by way of securing the reputation of his work.

[a] See the Credibility of the Gospel History, by the laborious Dr. Lardner: Part II. Vol. III. p. 31—35. and Vol. IV. p. 687—699.

3. This

3. This imprudence of Caius was not single in its kind, but was followed by another, which happened, on much the same occasion, in the East. Nepos, an Egyptian Bishop towards the middle of the third century, had revived the licentious errors of Cerinthus, which had been lately patronized at Rome, and published a treatise, entitled a *Confutation of the Allegorists*, in which he had ridiculed the interpretations of those, who were for explaining the Millennium in a figurative sense. As, some how or other, this treatise of Nepos came into vogue, Dionysius, Bishop of Alexandria, undertook to give it a formal answer, in two books *Concerning the Promises*; in which, not content with refuting what Nepos had asserted in defence of the Chiliasts, he went so far as to shake the credit of the Apocalypse, on which all the reasoning, such as it was, of the Millenarians was built. But here we are to note, for the honour of the Alexandrian Prelate, that he had

something more both of sense and modesty than the Roman Presbyter: for he ventures not to deny that the book was written by a person inspired, or that such person was called John; but he contends, it was not John, the son of Zebedee and brother of James, the writer of the Gospel and of the three Epistles, but another of the same age and name, who lived at Ephesus in the lesser Asia.

As the arguments of Dionysius are in substance not unlike to what later writers have adduced, in proof of the same opinion; it will not be inexpedient to lay them briefly before you, and then to subjoin so much of what has been offered in reply to them, as seems to be solid and satisfactory.[t]

He tells us then, first of all, that there is a striking difference between the Gospel

---

[t] The arguments here mentioned are preserved in a fragment of Eusebius, (Histor. Ecclef. Lib. VII. c. 24, 25) and are translated into English, in the 4th Vol. of the 2d Part of Lardner's Credibility, &c. in the History of Dionysius of Alexandria.

and

and Epistles, universally ascribed to John the son of Zebedee, and the Apocalypse, which alone creates a suspicion that all the three were not composed by the same person; the author of the former having never once in any of those writings inserted his name; but the author of the latter not only prefixing his name to the beginning of his book, but repeating it in other places more than once. This suspicion is strengthened from observing that the John, who is so careful to record his name in the Revelation, has not any one of those characteristic marks, which distinguish the person of the Evangelist; such as being *the disciple whom Jesus loved*, who *leaned on his breast at supper*, and one of them *who saw and heard the Lord*; all which circumstances are related, or referred to, both in the Gospel and the Epistles. Again, between these last there is a manifest conformity, in the sentiment, and in the expression; which plainly shews that both proceeded from the same author;

author; but the Revelation is altogether different from them, and bears not the least affinity or resemblance to either. Nor is there the most distant allusion in the Revelation to the Gospel or Epistles; nor in these to the Revelation; which in works of the same person was to be expected. And lastly, there are many inaccuracies and idiotisms of language in the Apocalypse; none of which are to be found in the acknowledged productions of John, the brother of James.

But the answer to these objections is easy. The argument drawn from the name of the author being often inserted in the Revelation, and always omitted in the Gospel and Epistles, is overthrown, by remarking that other Evangelists besides St. John have neglected to add their names to the Gospels which they published; and as to the Epistles, they, to whom they were addressed, could not be ignorant from whence they came. With respect to the Apocalypse the case was different;

different; this is neither a Gospel, nor yet, wholly, an occasional Epistle, but a species of writing distinct from both, or, in other words, a Prophecy: here therefore, after the example of the old Prophets, and especially of Daniel, whose manner he professedly imitates, it became him to prefix and to repeat his name; in order to give credence to his predictions, and that posterity might know to whom they were indebted for so wonderful a discovery of the fortunes of the church of Christ.

This remark will help to shew the futility of what Dionysius further urges, that none of the incidents of the Evangelist's life are told in the Revelation: for, besides that such an enumeration was now unnecessary from the mention already made by the writer of his name, he has actually said enough to point out, without any uncertainty, who he was, by directing part of his book to the seven churches of the proconsular Asia, over which

which St. John is known to have presided; and by describing himself as having been banished to Patmos, for the sake of his religion; a calamity, which, by the consent of all the ecclesiastical historians, confessedly happened to our Evangelist. As to the diversity of phrase and sentiment, in the Revelation and the other writings of St. John, it has been satisfactorily proved that this difference is not near so great as Dionysius would represent it; no greater than what may fairly be accounted for from the difference of subject; and particular instances have been alleged, in which there is a remarkable coincidence both of ideas and words, which are peculiar to this Apostle, and no where used by any other writer of the New Testament.

That the Revelation does not allude to the Gospel or Epistles; nor these again to the Revelation, can be of little moment, when we reflect, that though it be not unusual for one who writes to the same

same perſons more than once, to take notice of former letters addreſſed to them; yet in other treatiſes, directed to different perſons, on different occaſions, and at diſtant times, ſuch alluſions are not only rare, but would alſo in moſt caſes be unintelligible. And laſtly, with regard to the inaccuracies of language, which, it is ſaid, abound in the Apocalypſe, it may be queſtioned whether theſe are ſo numerous as has been pretended; nor ſhould it be forgotten that ſome of the ableſt interpreters have vindicated, as faultleſs, and even as beauties of compoſition, what by others, leſs judicious or leſs informed, have been condemned as barbarous and ungrammatical ſoleciſms.

4. Still we ought not to omit to mention, that the fame of two ſuch perſons as Caius and Dionyſius contributed but too much, among the Greek Fathers more eſpecially, to leſſen the eſtimation of this prophecy; and that in ſome catalogues of the books of Scripture that were

were published in the fourth and fifth centuries, particularly the catalogue of the council of Laodicea, the Revelation is not found. But here it may be of use to recollect, that the opinions of those, who lived at so late a period, can never supersede the testimony of others, who flourished near the very times when the Apocalyptical visions were first committed to writing. Nor will the omission of this book in certain lists of canonical Scripture occasion any difficulty, when you are told that the express design of those lists was to enumerate such parts of the sacred code as were proper to be read in public, for the edification of Christian assemblies; for which the general obscurity of the Apocalypse, and the small concern it seemed to have with the state of the church in those days, rendered it unfit. It were easy also to reckon up a number of persons, of unsuspected integrity, who, during this period, set their seal to the Revelation, as the legitimate production

production of St. John: but, not to multiply names, the declaration of Sulpicius Severus, an historian of credit at the beginning of the fifth century, shall serve instead of all the rest; to whom the arguments for the truth and divinity of this important portion of Scripture were so convincing, that he hesitates not to tax those who did not retain it as guilty of the double offence of folly and impiety [u].

5. As we descend lower down to the sixth and following centuries, a different face of things presents itself: only one writer among the Latins, and a very few among the Greeks, are recorded, as having any remaining doubts either of the writer or the authority of the Apocalypse; and after the tenth century, the whole

[u] Interjecto deinde tempore, Domitianus, Vespasiani filius, persecutus est Christianos: quo tempore Johannem Apostolum atque Evangelistam in Pathmum insulam relegavit; ubi ille, arcanis sibi mysteriis revelatis, librum sacræ Apocalypseos, qui quidem à plerisque aut *stulte* aut *impie* non recipitur, conscriptum edidit. Hist. Sacr. l. ii. cap. 31.

controversy was dropt. What is more extraordinary still, the book itself, whether on account of the darkness of its subject, or of the wild and fanciful attempts that had been made to explain it, gradually sunk into oblivion: and in this state it was likely to have continued, had not the revival of letters at the Reformation, together with the accomplishment of some of the predictions concerning Antichrist, which that event had developed, brought this prophecy again into view, and occasioned a more accurate study of it by divines both of the Protestant and Papal parties. Yet even in these latter times, there are not wanting some, and those among the most respectable of either communion, who have recalled the ancient scruples about its authenticity. It will be enough to specify two, Erasmus, and Martin Luther. But the former of these professes in the strongest terms his belief that the book was written by one

divinely

divinely assisted [w]: and the latter, though, with the usual bluntness of his temper, he at first rejected the Apocalypse entirely, as neither apostolical nor prophetical, yet afterwards grew more sober and moderate on this head; and all his uncertainty, like that of Erasmus, was confined to the person of the author [x].

[w] De Apocalypsi diu dubitatum est, non dico ab hæreticis, sed ab orthodoxis viris; qui scriptum tamen ut à Spiritu Sancto profectum amplectebantur, de Scriptoris nomine incerti. Erasmi Opera, Tom. ix. p. 867. Edit. Cleric.

Dubitamus de auctore libri Job, et librorum Regum; nec ob id vacillat illorum auctoritas. Dubitamus de auctore Evangelii secundum Marcum; nihilo secius est illius sacrosancta apud omnes auctoritas.—De Apocalypsi jam decies respondi. Commemoro—diversorum sententias, sed ingenue fateor me submittere sensum meum judicio Ecclesiæ; cujus auctoritas nisi me moveret, plane confirmarem illud opus non esse Joannis Evangelistæ. Ibid. p. 1170.

[x] In libro Apocalypseos patior quemque uti judicio suo, nec meæ sententiæ quenquam adstrictum volo: tantum dicam quod sentio; non una est ratio quæ me coegit, ut neque Apostolicum neque propheticum librum esse crederem.
Vide Prolegomena Westenii in N. T. p. 181.

SERM. VII.

On the whole, if the universal and uncontroverted admission of any book, soon after its delivery, and its subsequent reception by the Christian church, when doubts and difficulties had now been raised concerning it, are of any use in fixing its authority; we have all this and more to induce us to retain the Apocalypse, not only as a genuine portion of holy writ, but also as the peculiar composition of that Apostle and Evangelist, whose name it bears. It has been no uncommon case for men, warmly addicted to a set of notions, to venture to set aside the most unquestionable parts of Scripture, which could not be made to quadrate with their preconceived opinions. Who knows not that the same Luther, who decided so rashly of the Revelation, and other Antinomians after him, discarded the Epistle of St. James, because they could not reconcile his doctrine of *Justification by Faith* with what was taught

on

on that important subject by St. Paul? The like observation may be made with respect to the Epistle to the Hebrews, the Gospel of St. Matthew, and even the Gospel of St. John. In the mean while, the advocates of the Church of Rome may do well to remember, that whatever objections on this matter may be started by Christians of other persuasions, *they* at least have no cause to triumph; since it is an article of faith with them that the Revelation of St. John constitutes an essential part of the sacred canon; and the only dispute between them and us is concerning the design and object of this momentous prophecy.

II. As a proper conclusion of this discourse, I will here add a few reflections on the TIME in which the Apocalypse was written. This question is of no small consequence to the right understanding of the book itself. If, as Grotius and Sir Isaac Newton maintain, it was composed in the times of Claudius or Nero, that is, is, *before* the destruction of Jerusalem by the Romans; it is natural to expect that such a memorable conversion of human affairs, as that event brought along with it, would not be unnoticed in this prediction: on the contrary, if, as the truer opinion seems to be, its date be determined to the reign of Domitian, that is, *after* the Jewish wars were over, then the conclusion is, that the explanation of the prophetic visions must be fetched from the history of later ages [y].

Now if the most ancient tradition of the Christian Church be of any use in settling a matter of this sort, the controversy may be decided very speedily. The earliest of those, who mention the Time of writing the Revelation, is Irenæus; and he declares, in the most precise and peremptory terms, that it was " seen no

---

[y] See Lardner's Credibility, Vol. XIII. p. 354—377. Wolfii Curæ Philologicæ, Tom. V. 373—384. Vitringa in Apoc. (cap. i. ver. 2.) p. 6—9. Daubuz on the Rev. p. 80, 81.

" long

"long time agoe, and almoſt in his own age, at the end of the reign of Domitian." One cannot ſuſpect this venerable Father of a deſigned falſhood, in a cauſe where he was under no temptation to prevaricate, and in a fact where it is morally impoſſible he ſhould be deceived; as, whatever computation we follow, the event of its publication cannot be removed to any great diſtance from his own time, and he muſt have had frequent opportunities of knowing the truth from the contemporaries of St. John himſelf. With the teſtimony of Irenæus that of Euſebius, both in his Chronicle and Hiſtory, of Jerom, of Sulpicius Severus, and many others, agrees. The only perſon, who differs from them, is Epiphanius; a writer at the expiration of the fourth century, who is far from exact on other occaſions in reporting the ſentiments of thoſe that lived before him, and particularly inaccurate in diſtinguiſhing dates and times. Yet what will not the love of system effect? It is on his single assertion, unsupported by the smallest degree of proof, and opposed by the united evidence of every author of reputation in that period, that Grotius chuses to rely, in fixing the Apocalyptic epoch to the reign of Claudius.

But Grotius, as if himself not satisfied with the bare word of Epiphanius, endeavours to confirm it with reasoning of his own; and with this view quotes a passage from Scripture, in which we are told, that *Claudius commanded all Jews to depart from Rome*[z]. Under the appellation of Jews, he thinks that Christians also were comprehended; and the example of the Emperor at Rome would *undoubtedly*, so Grotius says, be followed by many governours of the Provinces. But all history is unanimous in affirming, that the first Roman Emperor, who persecuted the Christians, was Nero. Claudius, his predecessor, did indeed, as we learn from

[z] Acts xviii. 2.

the Acts of the Apostles, by his Imperial Edict order the Jews to leave the city of Rome; and perhaps the Christians too might be removed together with them: but from the same Acts it appears, that in the Provinces both Jews and Christians were permitted to live without any molestation. Thus Paul and Silas are said to have dwelt quietly at Corinth, and to have attended the Jewish Synagogue there [a]: and the same tranquillity is observed to reign among the Church at Ephesus [b]. Nor is there the slightest vestige in the monuments of antiquity from whence it can be traced, that so much as a single Christian, who lived out of Rome, was banished by Claudius, and much less banished for the sake of his religion.

But the opinion of the early date of the Apocalypse has found a more illustrious patron than even the learned Gro-

---

[a] Acts xviii. 1. 4.
[b] Acts xix. 1. 8. 10.

tius:

tius. The incomparable Sir Isaac Newton[c] has been at the pains of composing a laboured argument to prove, that the banishment of St. John into Patmos, and consequently his writing of the Revelation, happened in the time of Nero. And it is but treating this great author with the reverence that is due to him, not to dismiss his hypothesis without some consideration.

First then Sir Isaac observes, that although " Eusebius, in his Chronicle and " Ecclesiastical History, follows Irenæus, " yet *afterwards* in his Evangelical De- " monstrations he joins the banishment " of John into Patmos, as does also Ter- " tullian, with the deaths of Peter and " Paul." But here this excellent man forgot, that the Evangelical Demonstrations of Eusebius were composed *before* his Ecclesiastical History, as is evident from that History itself. Nor does it ap-

[c] Observations on the Prophecies of Daniel and the Apocalypse, Part II. Ch. i. p. 235—246.

pear, from confulting the places referred to, that either Eufebius or Tertullian intended to fix the exact time of the fuffering and deaths of thefe three perfons; or that their feveral calamities overtook them during the life of one and the fame Emperor. Peter and Paul might fuffer martyrdom at the end of the reign of Nero, and St. John be banifhed at the end of that of Domitian, in perfect confiftency with all that is related by thofe two Fathers.

Sir Ifaac goes on—" The fame Eufebius
" mentions a ftory from Clemens Alexan-
" drinus concerning a youth, whom John,
" *after* his return from banifhment, com-
" mitted to the care of a bifhop of a certain
" city; with other particulars which could
" not be tranfacted but in many years, and
" require that John fhould have returned
" from Patmos rather at the death of
" Nero than at that of Domitian." But here again, in the original account of this matter, if indeed the ftory be any thing

more

more than a moral apologue, the Apostle is said to have been at the time far advanced in age; and supposing him only to have lived two or three years after he came from Patmos, there will be room enough for all the events of Clemens' narration to have their full completion.

I pass over what this respectable writer adduces from such historians as Pseudo-Prochorus, and the inventer of the fable that John was put by Nero into a vessel of hot oil and came out unhurt; and also from Arethas, a commentator of the sixth century; the two former as deserving of no credit, and the latter as coming too *late* to be admitted a competent judge of this question: and I proceed to what he alleges next concerning " the tradition of " the churches of Syria, preserved in the " *title* of the Syriac version of the Apo- " calypse; which title sets forth, that the " Revelation was made to John in Pat- " mos, where he was banished by Nero " the Cæsar." Now to this it may be replied,

replied, first, that the age of the Syriac version is very uncertain; secondly, that in that version there are many errors, with respect to the titles of the books of the New Testament; and thirdly, that the tradition of the churches of Syria can be of no use, because they did not generally acknowledge the Apocalypse for canonical scripture.

The last argument of this celebrated person, and on which, as peculiarly his own, he lays the greatest stress, is this: " The Apocalypse is *alluded* to in " the Epistles of Peter and in that to the " Hebrews; and therefore must have " been written *before* them." And allowing these allusions to be real, and to have been intended, there can be no doubt, not only that the reasoning of this great man would be conclusive, but also that a new proof would arise for the authority of the Revelation; as other Apostles must then be acknowledged to have referred to it in their writings. But the phrases, selected from the Epistle to the Hebrews

Hebrews and the first of St. Peter, are, by the confession of Sir Isaac himself, at the best obscure; some not at all corresponding in sense to those of the Revelation, others plainly taken from the prophecies of the Old Testament, from whence the Apocalyptical expressions are also borrowed. With regard to the second Epistle of Peter in particular, which, it is said, seems to be throughout a continued commentary on the Apocalypse; I cannot but be of opinion, that, if any allusions to this work had been designed, both the author and his book would have been mentioned with the same clearness that is used in the case of St. Paul, whose name St. Peter formally quotes, and whose writings he seriously recommends, at the end of this very Epistle.

Lastly, it remains to be observed, that besides the external arguments from tradition, there are also internal proofs in the Revelation itself, that it could not make its first appearance during the reigns of Claudius

Claudius or Nero, but at a later period. At the time of writing the Apocalypse, Churches had not only been established in the most considerable places of the lesser Asia, but several of them had undergone a variety of changes and revolutions, which do not arise but after a long tract of time. The Church of Ephesus had degenerated from her *first love* [d]; that of Laodicea had become *lukewarm*, and knew not that she was *miserable and poor and naked* [e]. Now St. Paul is supposed to have written his Epistle to the Ephesians about the ninth year of the reign of Nero; and in that Epistle, so far from reproaching them for the want of love or charity, he commends both their charity and their faith [f]: nor are there any marks of the Laodiceans, of whom the same Apostle speaks in his Letter to the Colossians [g], having relaxed into that state of indiffer-

[d] Rev. ii. 4.
[e] Rev. iii. 16, 17.
[f] Ephes. i. 15.
[g] Coloss. iv. 13. 15, 16.

ence,

ence, complained of in the Apocalypse. Again, from the Epistles directed to the Asiatic Churches it is evident, that the Christians had been harrassed with long and grievous troubles: the tribulation and poverty of the Church of Smyrna [h] is recorded; and honourable mention is made of Antipas, a faithful Martyr, who was put to death at Pergamos [i]. These things could, none of them, have place in the times of Claudius or Nero; the former of whom never molested the Christians at all, and the cruelty of the latter was confined to the metropolis of the Empire. The next persecutor, after Nero, was Domitian; and his barbarities, we are certain, were indiscriminately exercised at Rome and in the Provinces: by *his* order therefore it must have been, that St. John was banished to Patmos, *for the word of God and for the testimony of Jesus Christ* [k];

[h] Rev. ii. 9.
[i] Rev. ii. 13.
[k] Rev. i. 9.

where

where he was illuminated with the divine Spirit, and favoured with thofe heavenly vifions, the defign and meaning of which to attempt to unfold, fhall be the bufinefs of the three following Lectures.

SERMON VIII.

The Order and Connexion of the Visions of the Apocalypse.

Rev. i. 19.

Write the things which thou haſt ſeen, and the things which Are, and the things which Shall Be Hereafter.

IN order to attain right conceptions of the conſtitution of Nature, as laid before us in the volume of Creation, we are not to aſſume hypotheſes and notions of our own, and from them, as from eſtabliſhed principles, to account for the ſeveral phænomena that occur; but we are to begin with the effects themſelves,

and

and from these, diligently collected in a variety of well-chosen experiments, to investigate the causes which produce them. By such a method, directed and improved by the helps of a sublime geometry, we may reasonably hope to arrive at certainty in our physical enquiries, and on the basis of fact and demonstration may erect a system of the world, that shall be true, and worthy of its author. Whereas, by pursuing a contrary path, our conjectures at the best will be precarious and doubtful; nor can we ever be sure that the most ingenious theories we can frame are any thing more than a well-invented and consistent fable.

With the same caution we are to proceed in examining the constitution of Grace, as unfolded to our view in the volume of Redemption. Here also we are not to excogitate conceits and fancies of our own, and then distort the expressions of holy writ, to favour our misshapen imaginations; but we are first to advert to what God has actually made known of himself in the declarations of his word; and from this, carefully interpreted by the rules of sound criticism and logical deduction, to elicit the genuine doctrines of revelation. By such an exertion of our intellectual powers, assisted and enlightened by the aids which human literature is capable of furnishing, we may advance with ease and safety in our knowledge of the divine dispensations, and on the rock of scripture may build a system of Religion, that shall approve itself to our most enlarged understandings, and be equally secured from the injuries and insults of enthusiasts and unbelievers. On the other hand, previously to determine from our own reason what it is fit for a being of infinite wisdom to do, and from that pretended fitness to infer that he has really done it, is a mode of procedure that is little suited to the imbecillity of our mental faculties, and still less calculated to lead us to an adequate com-

comprehension of the will or works of heaven.

If this sober and modest spirit be necessary, when we are engaged in the study of the inspired writings in general, it is yet more necessary to be cultivated, when employed in the contemplation of the prophetic writings in particular. The misfortune, or rather fault, of most persons here has been, not so much to explore, from an attentive perusal of these mysterious oracles, what the mind of the prophet must be, as to collect, in consequence of certain *data* laid down beforehand, what may confirm and justify their own conceits. To this cause it is to be attributed, that every new interpreter has usually provided himself with a new hypothesis; which, being founded, like those of his predecessors, on no better support than the art and address of the contriver, has in its turn been quickly superseded or overthrown by the abilities of more expert, though perhaps

haps equally presumptuous, adventurers. Whereas the only way, which prudence and good judgement recommend to be observed on this subject, is to divest ourselves of all prejudices and pre-conceptions whatsoever; to find, if we can, from internal marks, what is the purpose and scheme and method of the predictions we would examine, and on these, now at length discovered, to fix the root and bottom of our interpretation. By this means, our explanations, be they what they may, not being built on principles arbitrarily taken up at pleasure, but derived from the nature and constitution of the work explained, will have in them all the soundness and stability of science; from which no subsequent expositor will have a right to depart, unless he can shew, from intrinsic evidence, either that the principles assumed are false, or not fairly deducible from the construction of the prophecies.

To

To apply these reflections to the case of the Apocalypse, to the consideration of which the course of this Lecture hath carried us. Who has not heard of the various and opposite contrivances that have been formed, to unravel the intricacies of this sacred book? almost all of which, however finely imagined or skilfully executed, have nevertheless by men of true discernment been rejected, as nothing more than amusing and entertaining fictions. And the reason is plain: almost all the authors of these different opinions have gone on one common error; bringing along with them an interpretation already prepared, and on that supposed interpretation attempting to ascertain the meaning of the several parts; instead of being at the pains of learning, from observation and enquiry, in what method, and by what kind of argumentation, that meaning must, if ever, be satisfactorily disclosed. It was not thus that the illustrious Joseph Mede proceeded, when

SERM. VIII.

when he attempted to penetrate the veil that till his time had enveloped this venerable prediction. He saw the extravagance and folly of former critics; and that it was necessary in the first place, renouncing all conjectures and hypotheses, to consult the Revelation itself, and to try if from that he could not trace sufficient tokens, purposely inserted by the holy Spirit, by which the series and connexion of the Apocalyptic visions might be found. He would admit of no objections to this scheme, but such as arose from the frame and structure of the prophecy, and not from any pre-supposed way of expounding it: he would let nothing pass for demonstration, but what was undeniably proved to be such from undoubted notes, included in the words and letter of the composition: he had the requisite patience as well as sagacity; and by a steady adherence to this severe and rigorous plan, he obtained, after many difficulties and delays, the knowledge

ledge he was in search of, and effectually secured his own inventions against the disgrace of being disproved or weakened by the labours of future commentators.

I propose, in what follows of this discourse, to lay before you, as succinctly and yet as clearly as I can, the manner of opening the book of the Revelation, as it is explained at large by this great author in what he calls his *Apocalyptic Key* [1]; and to point out, in a regular progression, the steps, by which, as is probable, he was led to this important discovery.

I. First then it appears, from the most superficial view of the Apocalypse, that it is made up of Two component parts; one of which contains the Epistles to the Seven Churches of Asia, and is comprized within the three first chapters; the other foretells, as we say, the fortunes of Christianity, through the several periods

[1] See Mr. MEDE's Works, B. III. p. 419—432.

SERM. VIII.

of its primitive, degenerate, and reformed states, to its perfect consummation in glory, from chapter the fourth to the end. The former of these, being wholly relative to the condition of the Christian Church at the time of the vision, or, as the text expresses it, describing the THINGS WHICH ARE, falls not within our present subject: only it may be of use to remark in passing, that there are, who, not satisfied with the *literal* acceptation of these Epistles, have supposed them also to have a *mystical* meaning, and as well the names of the seven Churches, as the Churches themselves, to be typical of so many epochas, successive one to the other, in like manner as the Seals and Trumpets, afterwards described in this book. It would be easy to shew, from the most convincing arguments, that this opinion, which was first only hinted, in the way of query, by Mr. Mede [m], and was afterwards pursued at large by the ingenious

[m] See his Works, p. 905.

Henry

Henry More [n], is destitute of all solid foundation: and I mention it to shew, that it is one instance in which the scheme of this learned man has been pushed too far by some of his zealous admirers, who, as is usual with men of warm imaginations, have here indulged to their own fancies, without any proper support from Scripture.

II. Leaving then all that relates to the Asiatic churches, as foreign to the business of this Lecture; I go on to observe in the next place, that the Second Division of the Apocalypse, which is wholly prophetical, or, in the words of the text, descriptive of the THINGS WHICH SHALL BE HEREAFTER, may itself be resolved

---

[n] See his Theological Works, translated into Latin; among which is what he calls Expositio Prophetica Septem Epistolarum ad Septem Ecclesias Asiaticas, p. 781—824. For a confutation of this Exposition, the reader may consult the very learned Commentary on the book of the Revelation by Mr. Daubuz; note D. on Ch. i. 11. note B. on Ch. i. 19. note C. on Ch. ii. 10. Or the Dissertations on the Prophecies by Bp. Newton, vol. iii. p. 26, 27.

into

into two separate Tomes or Volumes; one of which may be called the Prophecy of the SEALED BOOK, and extends from the 4th chapter to very near the conclusion of the 10th; and the other may be called the Prophecy of the LITTLE or OPEN BOOK, and reaches from the 8th verse of the 10th chapter to the end. That these are two complete and entire prophecies, may be proved from this circumstance; that the beginnings of both, as also that of the Vision of the Seven Churches, are set out by a peculiar phrase, never elsewhere repeated, of *a voice from heaven as it were of a trumpet talking* with St. John [o]: the holy Spirit plainly intending by this token to distinguish these visions from all the others, which are nothing more than members or constituent parts of the Three Principal ones, that form the body of the book.

[o] Compare Rev. i. 10. with iv. 1. and x. 8.

III. 1. Having

III. 1. Having thus determined the beginnings and endings of thefe two leading prophecies of the Revelation, let us now fee, what are the Contents of each. And here it is evident, that the prophecy of the *Sealed Book* confifts of feven diftinct periods, expreffed by feven Seals, opened at feven different times, to every one of which is afcribed a character of its own. The character of the firft Seal is Victory [p]; that of the fecond is Slaughter [q]; that of the third is a Balance [r]; of the fourth is Death [s]; of the fifth is an Altar, having *under* it *the fouls of them that were flain for the word of God* [t]; and of the fixth is a great Earthquake [u]. After the defcription of the fixth Seal fhould regularly follow that of the feventh; but between thefe two is interwoven, epifodically as it were, a vifion of *a hundred and forty four thoufand* out *of all the tribes of Ifrael*, who were to be *fealed in their*

[p] Rev. vi. 1—3. [q] Ver. 4. [r] Ver. 5, 6.
[s] Ver. 7, 8. [t] Ver. 9—12. [u] Ver. 12—17.

foreheads, or preserved from amidst the ruins, now ready to take place under the last, or seventh, Seal [w]. This seventh Seal is of much longer duration han any of the rest; and is distributed into seven parts, marked by the sounding of seven Trumpets [x]. At the sounding of the first Trumpet, Hail is cast upon the Earth [y]; at the sounding of the second, a burning Mountain is cast into the Sea [z]; at the sounding of the third, a Star falls upon the Rivers [a]; the fourth Trumpet is attended with an Eclipse of the Sun, Moon, and Stars [b]; the fifth is followed by Locusts coming out of the bottomless pit [c]; the sixth by four Horsemen loosed from Euphrates [d]; and at the seventh, or last, Trumpet, *the kingdoms of this world become the kingdoms of our Lord and of his Christ* [e], at which time *the mystery of*

---

[w] Rev. Ch. vii.   [x] Ch. viii. 2.
[y] Ch. viii. 7.   [z] Ch. viii. 8, 9.   [a] Ver. 10, 11.
[b] Ver. 12, 13.   [c] Ch. ix. 1—12.
[d] Ch. ix. 13—21.   [e] Ch. xi. 15.

God

Visions of the Apocalypse.

God will *be finished, as he hath declared to his servants the prophets* [f]. This is, in short, a detail of the particulars, which constitute the prophecy of the Seals, the hidden meaning of which we are not now concerned to enquire into: only it will be of use to have it remembered here, that the series of *this* prophecy, and the series of the things predicted in it, is one and the same; that is, the things foretold are to follow one another in the same train as the Seals and Trumpets do; or, in other words, the events described, whatever those events may be, are, not concurrent, but successive.

2. We now proceed to examine the contents of the second great prophesy of the Revelation, namely that of the *Little* or *Open Book* [g]; considering it, at present, as an entire work of itself, without any dependance on the Book of the Seals. And here a very different face of things appears, from what was discernible on a

[f] Ch. x. 7.   [g] Ver. 8—11.

view of the former volume: a number of visions, represented under various and shifting symbols, is recorded, without any certain and determinate order, like that of the Seven Seals and Seven Trumpets; and which of them are antecedent or consequent, and which, if any, are collateral to the other, in point of time, is by no means evident at first sight. Here therefore our chief care must be to discover, from innate characters, whether any, and which, of the visions are of such a texture as, although disperfed (as was not possible to be avoided) in different parts of the prophecy, are yet really to be considered as coincident, or, in the language of Mr. Mede, *synchronical:* and when once the visions of this sort have been previously ascertained, it will then be no difficult matter, from the circumstances and progression of the history, to assign the order of the rest, according as they are seen to precede or follow those, whose

whose times and places have been already settled.

Now in this Little or Open Book there are FOUR Visions, which, it plainly appears, must all be transacted in *equal* times; and on examination it will appear, that these equal times must also be the *same*. The Visions alluded to are, The Treading or Profaning of the Outer Court of the Temple and of the Holy City by the Gentiles, for forty-two Months [h]; the Beast with Seven Heads and Ten Horns, which hath power given it for the same number of Months [i]; the Prophesying of Two Witnesses in Sackcloth, for a thousand two hundred and sixty Days [k]; and the continuance of the Woman in the Wilderness, during the same number of Days [l], or, as it is elsewhere expressed, during a *Time and Times and half a Time* [m]. All these several in-

[h] Rev. Ch. xi. 1, 2.
[k] Ch. xi. 3—19.
[m] Ch. xii. 14.
[i] Ch. xiii. 1—5.
[l] Ch. xii. 1—6.

tervals are equal to each other; for a Time and Times and half a Time, that is, as the phrase is explained, three Years and a half [n], make forty-two Months; and forty-two Months make 1260 Days, supposing the Year to consist of 360 days. But as the *equality* of times does not necessarily infer their *sameness*, or does not hinder but that some of the times may be prior or posterior to the other; this point may be demonstrated thus. The times of Profaning the Outer Court and City, and of the Prophesying of the Witnesses, are not only equal, but coincident, as is clear from the Revelation itself, and is confessed by all [o]: now the time of the Witnesses is coincident with

[u] Rev. xii. 6. 14.

[o] Ch. xi. 2, 3, compared with ver. 18, 19; where the same *Gentiles*, or *Nations*, who profane the Outer Court of the Temple, ver. 2, are described as *angry*, when the *two Witnesses have finished their testimony*, at the end of the sixth Trumpet, or *second woe*, ver. 7. 14, as being then expelled from their possession of the Temple.

that of the Ten-horned Beast; and the time of the Ten-Horned Beast is coincident with that of the Woman's abode in the Wilderness; as shall immediately be proved: but times, coincident with any third, are coincident with one another: therefore all the four times, of Profaning the Outer Court, of the Two Witnesses, of the Ten-Horned Beast, and of the Woman in the Wilderness, are also coincident; that is, the four Visions are all synchronical, or contemporize throughout. That the times of the Witnesses and of the Ten-Horned Beast, and those of the Ten-Horned Beast and of the Woman in the Wilderness, are the same, may be shewn thus. Equal times, which begin and end together, must of necessity be the same times: the times of the Witnesses and of the Ten-Horned Beast *end* together, namely, at the end of the sixth Trumpet p; therefore, being equal

p When the Witnesses finish their testimony, the Beast makes war against them and kills them.

times, they must begin together. Again, the times of the Ten-Horned Beast and of the Woman in the wilderness *begin* together, namely, after the victory of Michael over the red Dragon q; therefore, as before, being equal times, they must end together also.

Having cleared our way thus far, we may advance a step farther, and see whether there be not other visions in the prophecy of the Little Book, which

---

xi. 7. But they revive again, ver. 11, and ascend up to heaven in a cloud, ver. 12; and *in the same hour* an earthquake destroys the tenth part of the City, ver. 2. 13. On the arrival of this event, the second woe, or the sixth Trumpet, is represented as *past*, ver. 14; the seventh Trumpet sounds; and the kingdoms of this world, now no longer subject to the dominion of the Beast, become the kingdoms of our Lord and of his Christ, ver. 15.

q The Dragon being cast out of heaven by Michael, xii. 7, 8, 9, the Woman flies into the Wilderness, ver. 6. 14; where the Dragon makes war with the remnant of her seed, ver. 17, and gives his power and his seat and great authority to the Beast having seven heads and ten horns, that riseth out of the sea, xiii. 1, 2.

ought to be included in the same general Synchronism with the four mentioned above. Besides the Beast with Ten Horns, which is said to emerge out of the Sea, another with Two Horns is described, as at the same time coming out of the Earth [r]; which gives life to the Ten-Horned Beast, who is called its *Image* [s]; and is afterwards apprehended, and destroyed, together with it, both being *cast alive into a lake burning with brimstone* [t]: these two Beasts therefore, being inseparable one from the other, in their rise and in their extinction, must of course be considered as contemporaries. Again of the Ten-Horned Beast we are told, that its employment is to carry a Woman *arrayed in purple,* whose name is *Mystery and Babylon the Great* [u]: consequently this same Beast, and the Babylonish Woman

---

[r] Rev. xiii. 11.
[s] Ch. xiii. 15. xiv. 9. 11. xv. 2. xvi. 2.
[t] Ch. xix. 20. compared with xiii. 13, 14, 15, 16.
[u] Ch. xvii. 3, 4, 5. 7.

who *rides* it, must be contemporaries also. Lastly, collateral with the Babylonish Woman, is a Virgin-company of a hundred and forty-four thousand, whose office it is to denounce the future ruin of Babylon, and who are commended for preserving their fidelity to the Lamb at a time when the other inhabitants of the world had deserted to the service of the Beast [w]. As therefore the Virgin-company of one hundred and forty-four thousand synchronises with the Babylonish Woman, the Babylonish Woman with the Ten-Horned Beast, and the Ten-Horned Beast with the Beast with Two Horns; all four must synchronize with one another. But we have seen, that the Ten-Horned Beast is also synchronical with the Profaning of the Outer Court of the Temple, with the prophesying of the Two Witnesses, and with the abode of the Woman in the Wilderness. From

---

[w] Rev. xiv. 1. 4. 8. xvii. 2. 14. xviii. 3.

whence we come at this conclusion, that every one of the SEVEN Visions, that have been here related, are synchronical, or must all be comprehended within the same period of 42 Months, or 1260 Days.

And now, having established the synchronism of these Seven Visions, the places of those that remain will be determined very speedily. Of these there are TWO, namely, the Inner Court of the Temple, which St. John is ordered to measure [x], and the Battle of Michael and the Dragon concerning the Woman ready to be delivered [y], which, it appears from the narration, are the *immediate antecedents* of two of the Seven contemporary visions;—the Inner Court, for instance, immediately precedes, in situation and structure, the Outer, or ends where that begins; and the Battle of Michael and the Dragon concerning the Woman im-

[x] Rev. xi. 1, 2.
[y] Ch. xii. 3, 4. 7, 8. 13, 14.

mediately

mediately precedes the flight and abode of that Woman in the wilderness [z];—and therefore must be contemporary themselves. Again there are other TWO, which the sequel of the story shews to be plainly *subsequent* to the Seven Visions, before described; nor only subsequent to them, but coincident with each other. These are the effusion of the seven Vials [a], and the now impending falls of the Beast and of Babylon [b]. For it is asserted in so many words, that the design of the seven Vials was by so many successive plagues to punish the worshipers of the Beast [c]; and at the pouring out of the seventh, or last, Vial, Babylon is destroyed [d].

After the overthrow of the Beast and Babylon, the Dragon himself, who at the beginning of this Book was said to lye in wait for the Woman about to be delivered,

[z] Rev. xii. 4, 5, 6. 13, 14.
[a] Ch. xv.   [b] Ch. xvi.
[c] Ch. xv. 1, 2, 3. xvi. 2, 10.
[d] Ch. xvi. 17, 19.

and

and to have occasioned her flight into the desert [e], is shut up in confinement for a thousand years [f], during which interval the Saints live and reign with Christ [g]; and, coincident with this event, the New Jerusalem, in whose light the nations that are saved are to walk, comes down from heaven [h]. The Millenary state being expired, the Dragon, or Satan, is loosed from his prison; and, having exercised his fury *against the Saints and the beloved City* for a season, he is at length cast into utter perdition, by being thrown into the lake of fire and brimstone, *where the Beast and the false Prophet are* [i]. All the enemies of God and the Lamb being thus removed, nothing remains to finish the history of the Christian Church, but an account of the General Resurrection and Judgment of mankind, and the end of the

[e] Rev. xii. 4. [f] Ch. xx. 1, 2, 3. [g] Ch. xx. 4. [h] Ch. xxi. 2. 10. 24. [i] Ch. xx. 7. 9, 10.

World:

World [k]: and with this awful cataftrophe, announced with the greateft fublimity of figures and majefty of defcription, the Prophecy of the Little Book concludes.

IV. But we are not yet arrived at the full view of Mr. Mede's difcoveries: for not content with inveftigating the true order and feries of thefe Two Prophecies of the Revelation, confidered apart, he proceeded, in the fame fpirit of caution, to examine them together: nor was it long before his penetrating genius difcerned, that the latter prediction was indeed a regular repetition of what had been already delivered in the former, though in a different way; that both began from one common term, and, running over the fame period of time, met again at one common ending; and confequently that each was commenfurate with, and fo of admirable ufe to explain and illuftrate, the other. To this thought he feems to have been led from the words of the

[k] Rev. xx. 11, 12. xxii. 3, 4, 5.

Angel,

Visions of the Apocalypse.

SERM. VIII.

Angel, on delivering the Little or Open Book to St. John, *Thou must prophesy* AGAIN *before many peoples and nations and tongues and kings* [l]: and by following this hint, and setting the prophecies as it were side by side, he was enabled to trace the mutual habitudes and relations between the two, in the same way of synchronism, which he had applied with so much success to the latter, taken alone.

In considering the Two Prophecies of the Revelation with this view, it is obvious there is one vision, which is the *same* in both; namely, the company of one hundred and forty-four thousand, who are described as followers of the Lamb. In the Sealed Book, this vision is inserted immediately after the sixth Seal [m]; and therefore must belong to, and *begin with*, the seal next in order, or the seventh, consisting of seven Trumpets [n]: in the Open Book,

[l] Rev. x. 11.
[m] Ch. vii. Compare vi. 12. viii. 1.
[n] Ch. viii. 1, 2.

Book, it is one of the seven contemporary visions, which make a part of that prophecy [o]. Now by the help of this middle term we are able to prove, that the Seven contemporary Visions, in the Open Book, and the Six first Trumpets of the seventh Seal, in the Sealed Book, must of necessity be synchronical. For first, the *beginning* of those Seven Visions, and the beginning of the Six Trumpets, is the same: for all the seven contemporary visions must needs begin together; and one of these visions is the company of one hundred and forty-four thousand; and the beginning of *that* vision, we have just now seen, coincides with the beginning of the seventh Seal, which Seal is divided into seven successive Trumpets [p]. Secondly, the *end* of those Seven Visions, and the end of the Six Trumpets, is the same: for one of those visions is the Prophesying of the Two Witnesses [q]; and that the time of

[o] Ch. xiv.
[p] Compare vii. 1, 2. with viii. 1, 2.
[q] Ch. xi.

their prophesying and the time of the Sixth Trumpet end together, is plain from the express words of the Revelation; where after the death and resurrection of those witnesses it is subjoined, that *the second Woe*, that is, the Sixth Trumpet, (the three last Trumpets being called *Woe-Trumpets*) *is past, and the third Woe*, or the seventh Trumpet, *cometh quickly* [r]. Here then we may take occasion to admire the divine art and contrivance of this mysterious composition: for no reason can be assigned, why the vision of one hundred and forty-four thousand was suffered to disturb the course of the Sealed prophecy at all, by being inserted between the sixth and seventh Seals [s]; or why the account, of the ending of the sixth Trumpet and beginning of the seventh [t], which should

---

[r] Rev. xi. 7. 12. 14, 15.

[s] The sixth seal ends with ch. vi. the seventh seal, with its seven trumpets, begins ch. viii. Between these two is interposed the vision of one hundred and forty-four thousand, ch. vii.

[t] Rev. xi. 14, 15.

regularly

SERM. VIII.

regularly have been given at the conclusion of the former prophecy, was yet reserved for the latter, to which it seems not properly to belong; unless the Holy Spirit, intending to point out the connexion of the Two Predictions, designedly disposed the two corresponding visions, of the company of one hundred and forty-four thousand [u] and of the prophesying of the Witnesses [w], in such a way, that they might serve as hinges, by which the Open Book should be hung, as it were, on the book of the Seals. For it is observable, that the sounding of the seventh Trumpet, which should have made the close of the Sealed Book, where the Trumpets are all contained, is only *intimated* there, by informing us, that whenever that sounding *should be,* the *mystery of God* would be *finished* [x]. But in the Open Book it is related in form; and related too in that very place, where in the order of the nar-

[u] Rev. vii and xiv.
[w] Ch. xi. 3—14.
[x] Chap. x. 7.

ration

ration we should naturally expect to find it; namely, after a succinct history of events, from the beginning of Apocalyptical time down to the period collateral with that where the prophesy of the Sealed Book was seen to end [y].

This cardinal synchronism being settled, the coincidence of the remaining parts of the Two Prophecies may be easily shewn. For from hence it follows, that the visions of the Inner Court and of the victory of Michael over the Dragon, which immediately precede the seven contemporary visions in the Open Book [z], and the Six First Seals, which immediately precede the Seventh, or, what is the same thing, the Six first Trumpets of the Seventh, in the Sealed Book [a], must likewise coincide. Again, the effusion of the Seven Vials, by which are represented so many degrees of the fall of the Beast, in

[y] Rev. xi. 15—19.
[z] Ch. xi. 1. and xii. 3. 7, 8, 9. 13, 14.
[a] Ch. vi.

SERM.
VIII.

the latter prophecy [b], muſt coincide with the Sixth Trumpet, with which the power of that Beaſt comes to an end, in the former [c]. Laſtly, the founding of the Seventh Trumpet, in one prediction [d], muſt correſpond with the Millennium and the new Jeruſalem, in the other [e]; theſe two ſets of viſions being the immediate ſubſequents to other correſponding ſets; and both being related as coming *before* the General Reſurrection [f], which conſtitutes the end of the book of the Revelation, and of the World.

V. After ſo long a detail of the conſtituent parts of the Apocalypſe, and of the ſubdiviſions and contents of each; I have only time to make two or three ſhort reflections.

1. Firſt then it has been ſeen, that notwithſtanding the apparent diſorder and confuſion

---

[b] Rev. xv, xvi.
[c] Ch. xi. 14. See the Note [r], p. 243.
[d] Ch. x. 7. and xi. 15.
[e] Ch. xx. 1—4. and ch. xxi.
[f] Ch. xx. 11—15. and ch. xxii.

confusion of this book, there are yet sufficient marks, not difficult to be discerned by those who study it with a pure mind, by which the series and connexion of the visions may be known, without and even against the supposal of any pre-determined interpretation. It has been further seen, that many of these visions bear about them internal characters of contemporaneity; but that, as in a History, where various particulars are to be described, which really happened at one and the same time, it is yet impossible to relate them all together, but some must unavoidably be written down *before* the other; so in this Prophecy, where various visions are to be recorded, which clearly respect one and the same period, they are nevertheless transcribed in the book itself, as if they were to be fulfilled in progression. Hence we have this conclusion, that all such interpretations, as are founded on the notion that the events foretold are to succeed one another in the same order as the visions, must be totally erroneous and false.

2. Secondly, As that part of the Revelation, which contains the future fortunes of the Church of Christ, consists of two distinct and separate prophecies, connected together by a peculiar artifice, that of Synchronism; whatever principle is assumed in order to explain these prophecies, it must bear the exposition quite through, and solve all the seeming contradictions purposely thrown in to obscure them, as the true key of a riddle always does; otherwise the principle itself, and the interpretation built upon it, will be fallacious and unsafe. Particular symbols and passages may be expounded by partial commentators with great plausibility, and even semblance of truth; but nothing short of an universal principle will clear up the whole of this prophetical enigma, or produce a full conviction in which the mind of a sagacious enquirer may acquiesce.

3. Thirdly,

3. Thirdly, if among the several Apocalyptic visions here delineated we should haply be able to find the meaning of any *one*; we may, by the help of that one, together with the right application of the synchronisms already demonstrated, investigate the hidden sense of the rest. For all the visions, that have been proved to contemporize with that, whose meaning we have now discovered, must of necessity be interpreted of contemporaneous events; the visions, preceding that one vision, must be referred to preceding events; and the visions, subsequent to it, must relate to other events that are to follow it.

4. Lastly, it remains to observe, that one such vision is actually explained to us by the Angel himself, who communicated the Revelation to St. John: and that is, the vision of the Babylonish Woman, riding on the Beast *with seven heads*: by which *seven heads*, we are told, are meant *seven mountains, and by the Woman is re-*
presented

presented that great City which, in the times of the Apostle, reigned over the kings of the earth [g]. Here then let us fix the ground and principle of our future disquisitions; and having the word of God, like another pillar of fire, for our guide, let us try to explore our way through the obscure and dreary places of this great wilderness: not doubting but the *Father of lights,* from whom *cometh every good and perfect gift* [h], will teach us by his Spirit to discern and embrace the truth; that we may *understand a proverb, and the interpretation, the words of the wise and their dark sayings* [i].

[g] Rev. xvii. 3. 9. 18.
[h] James i. 17.
[i] Prov. i. 6.

SERMON IX.

Vision of the Apocalypse concerning the Babylonish Woman.

REV. xvii. 18.

The Woman, which thou sawest, is that Great City which reigneth over the kings of the earth.

YOU may have seen an optical experiment, of the following kind. A painted board is produced, besmeared with colours, thrown together, as it were, at random, and in which are discernible no obvious marks of figure or design. When the spectator has surveyed, for some time, and not without disgust, this unmean-

unmeaning mixture of discordant tints; a cylindrical mirror is placed on the board, in a certain position; when behold, the dispersed and dislocated parts instantaneously arrange themselves into an entire and perfect whole, and an elegant form is reflected from the burnished steel, composed with nicest symmetry and art, and set off with all the grace and harmony of colouring.

The book of the Revelation to an unskilful or careless reader appears to lie in a state like that of the painted board; from which it seems impossible to extract any regular or connected system. But by applying to this mysterious volume, in the manner already explained, the contrivance, distinguished by the name of Synchronism, an effect is experienced similar to that from the polished mirror: the disorder, which was thought to predominate throughout, immediately vanishes; the several disjointed visions are judiciously disposed, so as to constitute an unity of subject;

subject; and this subject is prosecuted, from end to end, according to a constant and pre-established plan, which is never more curious and artificial, than when least suspected by an ignorant or inattentive reader.

But the discovery of the true scheme and method, pursued in the Apocalypse, would have been of little use, had not the same divine Spirit, who imparted these wonders to St. John, been pleased yet further to furnish him, and us, with a sure and unerring clue, by which we might be conducted, as through the windings of a labyrinth, to the right interpretation of this extraordinary composition. Such a clue we find in the chapter, of which the text is a part: for thus the Angel, after having exhibited to the astonished Apostle the vision of a *Woman, whose name, written on her forehead,* was *Mystery, Babylon the Great, the Mother of Harlots,* and riding upon a *Beast* with *seven heads and ten horns* [k], unfolds to him the meaning of this amazing sight; *The* SEVEN HEADS *are* SEVEN MOUNTAINS *on which the Woman sitteth; and the* WOMAN, *which thou sawest, is that* GREAT CITY *which reigneth over the kings of the earth* [l]. Let us presume then, but with religious awe, to develope the sense concealed under this sublime oracle, and draw out its secrets into open day: nor need we fear the attempt will be censured as profane, when we proceed under the auspices of an heavenly guide, who has condescended to perform himself the office of Hierophant, and to give us, in part at least, his own explanation of this venerable Mystery.

I. Now that by the City here represented, after the manner of the ancient prophets, under the symbol of a Woman, and distinguished by the appellation of Babylon, is to be understood ROME, is put

[k] Rev. xvii. 1. 3. 5.
[l] Ch. xvii. 9. 18.

beyond

beyond all manner of doubt, not only from what is said of the situation of this city, that it was built on *seven hills* [m], but from what is mentioned besides, that, at the time when St. John lived, it *reigned*, or had supreme dominion, *over the kings of the earth* [n]. For these two circumstances, taken together, are such appropriate and discriminative characters of the Metropolis of the Roman Empire, that they confessedly belong to it, and cannot both be shewn to belong to any other. Hence Papists, as well as Protestants, have been among the foremost to acknowledge, that this is indeed the place foretold.

II. Taking it then for granted, as we safely may, that the Babylon here described is no other than Rome; an important question arises, to what particular period of the existence of this city the prophecy before us refers? Now there are but two opinions, which can possibly have claim to our attention, in the solu-

[m] Ver. 9.   [n] Ver. 18.

SERM. IX.

tion of this difficulty. One is of those, who contend that Pagan or Idolatrous Rome, such as obtained many ages ago, during the government of the persecuting Emperors, is solely intended here: of which sentiment are the Papists almost universally, and some few among the Protestants. The other is of those, who, though they do not exclude Rome Heathen from all concern in the Apocalypse, yet maintain that its principal object is to predict the innovations, gradually introduced into the religion of Jesus, by Rome Christian and degenerate, such as it is seen at present under the government of the persecuting Popes. This is the sentiment generally entertained by Protestants: and it will be our business, in the sequel, to point out to you the reasons, which they are able to produce, in vindication of their persuasion.

Now it is certainly a strong *presumption*, that the antitype of Babylon is not Heathen Rome, that none of the Christians,

who

who lived and suffered under the oppressions of the Heathen Emperors, and who, one would think, would have been the quickest at discerning the resemblance, if there was any, between the prediction and its accomplishment, seem to have had the slightest suspicions, that themselves and their own fortunes were at all particularly interested in the sayings of this book: on the contrary, it is an historical fact, that they did not look for the tyrannical power, whose person and conduct are so minutely delineated by St. Paul and St. John, till the Roman Empire should come to its dissolution, and for this cause were frequent in their prayers to heaven, that such dissolution might be delayed. This, I say, is a violent presumption, against the validity of the former opinion related above, and in favour of the latter. However, as it may be replied, that the ancient Fathers might perhaps be aware of the true meaning of the prophecies, and yet, from motives of prudence, might chuse

chuse to appear reserved on a subject so delicate as that of the ruin of Eternal Rome: or even admitting they were ignorant of this matter, that a very natural account may be given of such their ignorance; their minds being too much engaged in the contemplation of their own misfortunes, to advert with accuracy to so obscure a part of scripture as the Apocalypse: nor is there any better ground for asserting that the Antichristian sovereignty, whose seat is allowed to be Rome, did not receive its completion in the persecuting Roman Emperors, because the Christians of those days did not see and own that completion; than there is for affirming that Jesus was not the expected Messiah, because the Jews, *before whose eyes* he was *evidently set forth* and *crucified* [o], did not acknowledge him as such?: for these reasons, I am not willing to lay greater stress on this observation

[o] Gal. iii. 1.
[p] Preface sur L' Apocalypse, par Bossuet, Eveque de Meaux, § 21, 22.

than

than it will bear; and am content to consider it as producing only a high degree of *probability*, that Babylon and Pagan Rome are not the same.

But now, if encouraged, not impeded, by this preliminary remark, we proceed to inspect, with care, the prophecy itself; we shall, if I mistake not, be no longer at a loss for arguments, to convert this high degree of probability into *proof*.

1. And the first thing which takes our notice is the name of *Babylon*[q], by which the holy Spirit hath distinguished the mystical Woman mentioned in the text. This city was undoubtedly selected, because known in the Jewish story as the author and supporter of Idolatry in the Heathen world, and therefore the fittest to typify the place, from whence the same corruption should originate in the Christian. But from this expression alone, it is granted, we cannot infer, that the object in view is Christian Rome.

[q] Rev. xvii. 5.

Another

Another name of the Woman, yet more infamous than the first, is that of *Whore*, with whom the kings of the earth have committed *Fornication*[r]. It is hardly necessary to remind you here, that the words *whoredom, fornication*, and the like, are the usual language of the old prophets, to denote the specific sin of idolatry: and though they be sometimes applied to Gentile cities, which had never entered into covenant with the one Creator of heaven and earth, their proper force consists in this, that the persons or nation, of whom they are predicated, had once engaged themselves, as it were by a marriage-contract, to the service of the true God, and had afterwards revolted to foreign deities[s]. But neither will this appellation perhaps, though less equivocal than the former, be thought by all persons to be decisive, that the prophet's rebuke is levelled against

---

[r] Rev. xvii. 1, 2. 5.
[s] See the xxxift Prelection on the sacred Poetry of the Hebrews by the learned Bishop of Oxford.

a corrupted Church, rather than a Pagan city.

What follows, it is presumed, will not be liable to any ambiguity. For, not content with branding the Woman with the title of Whore, the Angel informs St. John, that the turpitude implied in such a character would be aggravated yet further by her endeavouring to promote the same scandalous commerce in others; so that, over and above the guilt of being a Harlot herself, she would deserve to be called *the* MOTHER *of Harlots and abominations of the earth*[t]. This part of the description can with no propriety be accommodated to Rome, before it had embraced the faith of Christ; because, however addicted to the worship of idols that city may itself have been, during its unconverted state, it cannot justly be charged with labouring to spread the same infection among others. The very absurdities of Pagan theology rendered all

[t] Rev. xvii. 5.

attempts of this sort impracticable: for as every nation had a set of rites and ceremonies of its own, without the least interference with those of any other, the consequence was, an unlimited toleration among the different systems of Heathenism; each allowing the truth of the others pretensions, and none assuming a right to erect itself on the ruin of the rest. In the mean time it will not be denied, that Papal or Christian Rome is sedulously bent on nothing more, than on extending its religion with the same zeal the ancient Romans did their arms, and by the same methods too, even those of violence and persecution towards all opposers. This genius and disposition is emphatically marked in the phrase, MOTHER *of Harlots and Abominations of the* EARTH. The term of *Adulteress*, which, it is pretended, would here have been used, had Christian Rome been really signified, would have been inadequate to the occasion; nor would have expressed, with sufficient precision,

cision, the idea of that particular species of impurity, here meant to be conveyed; which is not so much that of a libidinous Wife, who violates her plighted faith to her own husband, as of a Woman, whose business and profession it is to solicit others to acts of uncleanness; who keeps as it were a public brothel, open to all comers, where she sits, with the attire and look of an Harlot, stretching out her *golden cup, full of abominations and filthiness of her fornication* [u], and practising her meretricious arts, to seduce the unwary passenger to his destruction.

2. The argument here advanced is strengthened not a little by what is afterwards remarked concerning the same Woman, that she was *drunken with the blood of the saints, and with the blood of the martyrs of Jesus*; on beholding which, the Apostle WONDERED *with great admiration* [w]. Now it could have been no matter of wonder to St. John, who saw and

[u] Rev. xvii. 4.   [w] Ver. 6.

felt the barbarities exercised by the Emperors Nero and Domitian, that Babylon should appear to him in the vision as Pagan Rome did to his bodily eyes. Nor can it now be matter of wonder to us, that the first disciples of Christ, who condemned the publick religion, established at Rome, of impiety, nor would consent to throw so much as a grain of incense on any of its altars, should for such inflexible obstinacy, as it was called, experience the edge of the severest sufferings. But that Christian Rome, a city professing subjection to the gospel of Jesus, which is averse to all the modes of compulsion and force, and wills only to gain admittance by the lenient arts of reason and persuasion; that such a city should so far forget or mistake the tendency of its own religious principles, as to become drunken, with blood, with Christian blood, *with the blood of the Saints and Martyrs of Jesus*; this argues such accumulated and prodigious guilt, as accounts for the

the *admiration* of the Apostle, and may well excite the astonishment of mankind.

3. But the character of the Woman in the text will be still better elucidated, by attending to what is said of the same person, in another part of the prophecy. In the 12th chapter we have a description of the Christian Church, in its purity; represented, as here, in a female form, but decorated with ornaments of a very superior kind: for she is *clothed with the sun*[x], encircled with the glorious light of the gospel of Christ, who is called the *sun of righteousness*[y] having the *moon under her feet*, trampling on the rudiments of this world, Jewish festivals and Gentile superstitions; *and upon her head a crown of twelve stars*, adhering stedfastly to the doctrine of the twelve Apostles. In this her primitive and heavenly state, whilst her pious labours

[x] Rev. xii. 1.   [y] Malachi iv. 2.

are

are directed to advance the kingdom of Chrift, fhe has to ftruggle with dangers on every fide, and is compaffed about with enemies, who are ever on the watch to deftroy her: which circumftances are typified by her *travailing in birth* and being *pained to be delivered* [z], and by the *red Dragon*, or the perfecuting Roman Empire, *ftanding before her, to devour her child as foon as born* [a]. However, through the controul of an over-ruling providence, the defigns of thefe her firft adverfaries are at length defeated; her pains, or the cruelties of the Pagan Emperors, are happily ended by her becoming the mother of a *man-child* [b], or by the gaining of a church from among the Gentiles: which child, or Gentile Church, being *caught up unto God and to his throne*, or being fafely lodged under the protection of the Roman Empire, now become Chriftian, fhe herfelf, like another Ifrael, makes her efcape into

[z] Rev. xii. 2.   [a] Ver. 3, 4.
[b] Ver. 5. 13.

the

the *Wilderness*[c], there to sojourn, for a limited number of years, and to be assailed with new troubles: with which account her history, in this chapter, ends.

In the chapter of the text, we meet with the same Woman again; and, to prevent all scruples concerning her identity, in the same *place*, where the conclusion of the above narration had left her, namely, in the *Wilderness*[d]:

> — But oh! how fall'n! how chang'd
> From her, who in the happy realms of light,
> Cloth'd with transcendent brightness, did outshine
> Myriads, tho' bright[e]!

For here we find her no longer clad, as when first *seen in heaven*[f], with the native glories of the celestial luminaries; but, instead of them, *arrayed in purple and scarlet colour, and decked with gold and precious stones and pearls*[g], or glittering with the tinsel of worldly grandeur; and in

---

[c] Rev. xii. 6. 14.   [d] Ver. xvii. 3.
[e] Milton, P. L. Book I. ver. 84, &c.
[f] Ver. xii. 1.   [g] Rev. xvii. 4.

this condition, like another Babylon, exerting the moſt illegal acts both of civil and ecclefiaſtic tyranny, and even glutting herſelf with the blood of thoſe, who dare to reclame againſt her enormous uſurpations. Nothing can more ſtrongly prove, that the Woman, in this laſt chapter, is the emblem of an apoſtate or corrupted Church, than the evidence which ariſes from the compariſon of theſe two viſions: the ſame perſon, it is obvious, is the ſubject of both: in one ſhe is deſcribed, as pure and undefiled, ſuch as befitted a religion, *coming down from the Father of lights*[h]; in the other, ſhe appears in a depraved and degenerate ſtate, ſuch as was to be expected in a Church, which had *left her firſt love*[i], and had contaminated herſelf with the double crimes of Idolatry and Perſecution.

4. If now we turn from the character of the Woman to that of the Beaſt, on

[h] James i. 17.   [i] Rev. ii. 4.

which

which she is said to *ride* [k], the same conclusion will meet us, though by a different way. The Woman herself having been already proved to be Rome, the Beast, that carries her, can be no other than the Roman kingdom. Indeed the properties attributed to this Beast, compared with those of the *fourth Beast* in the book of Daniel [l] (by which fourth Beast, we have seen, is signified the Roman government), are enough to shew, that the same government must also be denoted here. One of these properties, you may remember, is the having of *ten horns* [m]; which ten horns, we are told, are to be understood as signifying so many *kings* [n]: and as a further explanation, it is added by St. John, that these kings had *received no kingdom as yet* [o], or, at the time of the

---

[k] Rev. xvii. 3. 7.
[l] Dan. ch. vii.
[m] Dan. vii. 7. 20.
[n] Ver. 24.
[o] Rev. xvii. 12.

vision, were not in existence. Now it is notorious that the Latin or Western Empire was not dismembered, or broken into separate sovereignties, that is, the Beast was not possessed of its ten Horns, and consequently the Woman could not ride it in that state, till some considerable time *after* Rome had become Christian: whence arises this conclusion, impossible to be evaded by any sophistic interpretation whatsoever, that neither the Beast nor the Woman, in this part of the prophecy, can have any relation to Pagan Rome.

5. Lastly (for I am unwilling to press you with all the arguments that might be brought on this fruitful theme) the same persecuting power, which is represented here under the figure of a Beast with ten horns, is pourtrayed, elsewhere, under the image of another Beast, contemporary with the first, which had *two horns like a Lamb, and spake as a Dragon* [p].

[p] Rev. xiii. 11.

By the Lamb is uniformly meant, throughout the whole book of the Revelation, the person of Christ [q]: and this second Beast being otherwise characterized under the title of a *false prophet* [r], we learn that his lamb-like form was in appearance only, and that he was in reality one of those teachers described by our Lord, who *come in sheep's clothing, but inwardly are ravening wolves* [s]. The putting on of the semblance of a *Lamb* is an intimation that he would act in virtue of a pretended authority derived from Christ; at the same time his speaking as a *Dragon* leaves us in no doubt, that in heart and temper he would be a very Pagan. Hence therefore we have another proof, that the power in question, which by the acknowledgment of our adversaries is a Roman

---

[q] Rev. v. 6. 8. 12, 13. vi. 1. 16. vii. 10. 14. 17. xiii. 8. xiv. 4. xvii. 14. xix. 7. 9. xxi. 9. 27. xxii. 1. 3.

[r] Rev. xvi. 13. xix. 20. xx. 10.

[s] Matth. vii. 15.

power,

power, must of necessity be such a one, as in name and profession should own the faith of Christ, yet in fact should dishonour his religion by persecuting the best and sincerest of his followers.

III. On the whole, we may now have leave to assert, from internal marks to be found in the text itself, that the Babylonish Woman, whose features are here described, can only be understood of Papal or Christian Rome; such as it exists at present, corrupted in doctrine and manners, and polluted with spiritual whoredom, or Idolatry. This interpretation, however, you are not to be told, has not been without its opponents, of both communions, who have laboured to overthrow it: and it will be no improper close of this discourse to mention two expositions, contrary to that adopted here, and which, more for the eminence of their authors than for any solidity in themselves, may deserve to be noticed; I mean those

those of the learned Grotius, and the celebrated Bishop of Meaux.

1. The former of these illustrious persons, proceeding on the common error, that the main object of this prophecy is Heathen Rome, thinks he discerns, under the attributes of the Beast with seven heads, evident marks of the Roman government, as it subsisted in the times of Domitian[t]. This opinion, we must observe, is altogether founded on another, whose falsehood has been already demonstrated, that the Apocalypse was written during the reign of Claudius: for on supposition that the visions here recorded were not seen by St. John till the end of the reign of Domitian, the book, instead of being, as it assumes to be, a prediction of *things that should be hereafter*[u], will be nothing more than an history of facts, either past, or passing before the Apostle's eyes. There is another objection to the

[t] Annotationes ad Apoc. cap. xiii.
[u] Rev. i. 19. iv. 1.

hypothesis

hypothesis of Grotius: the persecution of Domitian was neither severe enough, nor long enough, to find a place in this prophecy: if the testimonies of Tertullian [w] and Lactantius [x] may be credited, the worst inflictions of this Emperor seem not to have extended beyond banishment; and, whatever they were, they certainly did not continue *forty-two months* [y], the time prescribed for the reign of the Beast; even allowing to this learned man, that these months are to be understood in their literal acceptation only.

2. The latter of the two expositors, spoken of above, was too sagacious not to perceive the faults, inseparable from

---

[w] Tentaverat et Domitianus, portio Neronis de crudelitate, sed qua et homo facile cœptum repressit, restitutis etiam quos relegaverat. Apol. Cap. v.

[x] Quam diutissime tutusque regnavit (Domitianus), donec impias manus adversus Dominum tenderet. Postquam vero ad persequendum justum populum instinctu Dæmonum incitatus est, tunc traditus in manus inimicorum luit pœnas. De Mort. Persec. cap. iii.

[y] Rev. xiii. 4, 5.

the system of Grotius; and was therefore compelled to vindicate the honour of his Church in another, and, to do him justice, a much more plausible way. He maintains, that the taking of Rome by Alaric the Goth, and, in consequence of that, the fall of Idolatry, is the one great subject of the Revelation: and that in order to realize the character of the Beast, we must have recourse to the reign of Diocletian, towards the conclusion of the third century; when the Roman Empire made its last and cruellest effort to extirpate the religion of Christ[z]. And so far must be granted, that no persecution, during the Pagan times, was carried on with greater severity, or has a better claim, on account of its continuance as well as barbarity, to be remembered, than this. But, as we have had occasion to observe on this argument before, it is not a specious resemblance that may be found be-

[z] Explication du Chapitre xiii de L'Apocalypse, par Bossuet.

tween one or two symbols and a few historical facts, which will satisfy a judicious reader of this book; but the discovery of some general and leading principle, that pervades, and is able to remove the difficulties of, the whole. Now to this the explication of the Catholic Bishop is plainly unequal. To give two instances, out of many. The ruin of the Beast is announced in these magnificent terms; *Babylon the Great is fallen, is fallen, and is become the habitation of devils, and the hold of every foul spirit, and a cage of every unclean and hateful bird* [a]. The expressions are taken from the Jewish prophets, in which the overthrow of the old Babylon is foretold; and, if words can convey any meaning, they can only be meant of such a destruction as is extreme and without remedy. And yet the Bishop of Meaux can suppose, that the force of this emblem is sufficiently exhausted in the shock, which the city of Pagan Rome received

[a] Rev. xviii. 2.

from

from the ravages of the Goths; though it be certain that city supported itself, and in tolerable vigour, after that event, under several successive Emperors. Again, at the sounding of the seventh Trumpet we are told, *the mystery of God will be finished, and the kingdoms of this world will become the kingdoms of our Lord and of his Christ* [b]; which prediction, according to the opinion of the same Prelate, was accomplished, in the conversion of the nations to Christianity, and the downfall of Heathenism, at the sacking of Rome by Alaric: though here also it be notorious, that Idolatry subsisted, in its full strength, in many countries then in alliance with Rome; and within no long time after, the impostor Mahomet arose, and diffused his errors far and wide, in avowed opposition to the gospel of Christ. Such interpretations rebel against common sense no less than against the evidence of authentic history; and are indeed proofs of nothing

[b] Rev. x. 7. xi. 15.

but

but the weakness of the cause they are brought to serve.

3. Lastly, Admitting the explanation of the vision in the 17th chapter, which has here been given, to be true, we are hence furnished with a certain method, by which the obscurities of the remaining visions, such I mean as have been already fulfilled, may be commodiously cleared. Thus, granting that the Babylonish Woman is rightly conceived to denote the city of Papal Rome; then the visions, which synchronize with this, must all be interpreted of such events, as are found in history to correspond with the times of Rome Christian; and the contemporary visions, antecedent to these, must all be illustrated from the history of the ages preceding, or falling in with the empire of Rome Pagan. Much has been done in this way by many commentators on the Apocalypse, who have appeared since the times of the Reformation; but by none, with greater caution and success, than by the

the incomparable Joseph Mede. And though even in him, such are the limits prescribed to the most comprehensive human understandings! there may perhaps have been discovered by later critics some few slight specks of natural infirmity, yet in the general principle on which he sets out, and the strict rules of demonstration by which he all along proceeds, he is so entirely without a flaw, that all who, under the notion of correcting, have presumed to differ from him here—I except not Sir Isaac Newton himself—seem more or less to have deviated from the truth, as they have more or less departed from his plan; and all that they have effected hath been only this, the doing of an undesigned honour to his discoveries.

SERMON X.

General Design of the remaining Visions of the Apocalypse.

Rev. xxii. 6.

These sayings are faithful and true; and the Lord God of the holy prophets sent his Angel, to shew unto his servants the things which must shortly be done.

SERM. X.

THERE are two ways, which we may legitimately pursue in our researches after natural knowledge: one is, from the qualities, which are found really to exist in bodies, to investigate the causes which produce them; from particular causes to ascend to general, till our enquiries arrive at the most general and

and terminate in first principles: the other is, to begin with these first principles themselves, and, descending from them by a regular series of proofs, to explain the obvious appearances of things. Of these methods it is evident that the former, which is founded on fact and observation, is to be first employed; and when by this kind of disquisition we have gained a sufficient number of truths, we may then, and not till then, securely have recourse to the latter. Thus Sir Isaac Newton, having demonstrated, first of all, that the power of gravity was diffused through every particle of matter on which experiments could be made, that it acted, according to an invariable law, on all bodies on and near the surface of the earth, that it extended to the moon, to the other planets, and to the sun itself; proceeded afterwards, in a reverse order, to illustrate, from the supposition of this principle, the visible system of the world, and to shew that, allowing

lowing such a force as gravity, the several phænomena of nature could not be otherwise than they are.

In like manner there are two ways, which we may safely follow in the prosecution of religious knowledge: one is, from internal characters, discernible in any given portion of God's written word, to try if haply we can find the general scheme and purpose of the writer: the other is, from that scheme and purpose, so discovered, to fix the signification of particular parts. It was thus, that Mr. Mede conducted himself in his endeavours to elucidate that obscurest of the prophetical volumes, the Revelation of St. John: having first, from the frame and texture of the work, established, analytically, the connexion and coincidence of the Apocalyptic visions, he afterwards perceived, that the meaning of one had been communicated by an heavenly messenger to the Apostle, and was by him inserted in his book: encouraged by this hint,

hint, he next adventured on the synthetic mode of reasoning, and setting out from that one vision, so interpreted, he attempted, and was enabled, to evolve the sense, which lay concealed under the rest.

It shall the business of the present Lecture to lay before you a succinct account of the several progressive steps, by which the celebrated writer now mentioned advanced, in order to remove the obscurity of the remaining parts of this prophecy, the order and arrangement of which he had previously settled. Such a view of the whole of Mr. Mede's inventions, with regard to this important portion of holy writ, will complete what is yet to be said on the subject of the Apocalypse; and will prepare you for hearing without surprize, what many even among believers have sometimes scrupled to admit, that the Revelation of St. John is indeed the most *methodical* book of Scripture.

The vision, alluded to above, is that of the Babylonish Woman; by which we have learnt, and from no less authority than that of an Angel, is prefigured the city of Christian Rome, now fallen from her primitive state of gospel purity, and defiled with the foulest stains of superstition and idolatry. Every vision therefore in the book, as has been already remarked, which may be clearly proved to contemporize with this of the Babylonish Woman, must of necessity be explained from the history of facts contemporary with Papal Rome. By this simple proposition it is, that all our future speculations must be regulated. Here then let us take our stand; and having gained the advantage of this rising ground, let us try if from hence, as from an eminence, we may not be able to survey the yet unknown region of the Apocalypse: not without first imploring the aid of that divine Spirit, of whose

office

office it is to *guide us into all truth* [d], that he would *open* the *eyes* of our understandings, that we may *behold wondrous things out of his law* [e].

I. It may be of use to remind you, that the Second great Prediction of the Revelation, which we have called the Prophecy of the Little or Open Book, contains, besides the vision of the Woman of Babylon, six other visions, coincident with it, in respect of time; namely, those of the Beast with seven heads and ten horns, the Beast with two horns like a Lamb, the profaning of the Outer Court of the Temple by the Gentiles; the prophesying of two Witnesses in sackcloth, the Virgin company of a hundred and forty-four thousand, and the flight and abode of the Woman in the wilderness [f]. Of these the first, or that of the ten-

[d] John xvi. 13.
[e] Pf. cxix. 18.
[f] See page 241—247.

horned Beast [g], it has been intimated to you in a former Lecture [h], is plainly descriptive of the Roman Kingdom: this is evident, as well from the known use of the general term *Beast* in the language of prophecy, which invariably denotes an idolatrous state or government, as from the particular properties ascribed to this Beast here; which are so exactly similar to those attributed to the fourth Beast in the seventh chapter of Daniel [i], as to evince beyond a doubt, that in both prophets one and the same power was intended. As little dispute need there be concerning the meaning of the second Beast, having *two horns like a Lamb, but speaking as a Dragon* [k]. The Lamb, we have seen [l], is the constant symbol of Christ; and this Beast being also denominated

---

[g] Rev. xiii. 1—10. xvii. 9—15.
[h] See page 279.
[i] See page 84—87.
[k] Rev. xiii. 11.
[l] See page 281.

minated a *false prophet* [m], and his acts being all of them calculated to promote the interests of a false religion (such as causing an image to be made to the first Beast, working miracles to seduce men to the worship of him, and even killing those who refuse to conform to his arbitrary decrees [n]); we are led to consider the power in question as partaking more of an ecclesiastical than civil nature, and corresponding in kind to that which we know to be actually exercised by the Roman Pontiff. Thus it appears that the visions of the Babylonish Woman and of the two Beasts were designed to exhibit, in succession, the several parts and members of that kingdom of Apostasy, whose rise and progress and decline are here foretold. Babylon, the mother of harlots, is the City of Rome, considered as the seat or metropolis of Antichrist; the Tenhorned Beast is the Roman Empire, after

---

[m] Rev. xvi. 13. xix. 20. xx. 10.
[n] Rev. xiii. 13, 14, 15.

it was divided into ten separate sovereignties, all subordinate to the capital city; and the Two-horned Beast is the presiding King or Magistrate of this degenerate society, invested with the habit of a secular tyrant, in virtue of his temporal acquisition of the patrimony of St. Peter, but essentially distinguished from every other earthly monarch, on account of his claims to spiritual dominion, and his usurped authority over the minds no less than the bodies of his deluded subjects.

Before we can explain the vision next in order, the profaning of the Outer Court of the Temple by the Gentiles [v], we must premise, that throughout the Revelation the fates of the Christian Church are recorded in words and phrases peculiar to the religion of the Jews, and particularly such as were appropriated to the ritual of the Temple-service at Jerusalem. Thus the Jews, or synagogue of the Israelites, who in the times of the

[v] Rev. xi. 2.

Mosaic

Mosaic dispensation were the only people that retained the knowledge of One God, are employed in this prophecy to personate the congregation of faithful followers of Christ, or those who are Christians indeed [p]; as the Gentiles, on the other hand, who in the days of Moses and the Law had universally relapsed into idolatry, sustain here the character of apostates, or those who have polluted the worship of the one Mediator between God and man with imaginary intercessors of their own. When therefore St. John was presented with a sight of the Outward, that is, the greater, Court of the Jewish Temple, which he was commanded not to *measure*, as he had the Inner or less Court, because it was *given unto the Gentiles*, who were to profane it for *forty and two months*; we are authorized from the received application of these symbols to interpret them as describing the condition of the visible Church

[p] Rev. ii. 9.

of Christ, now *given* for a certain time to be possessed by *Gentiles*, or made up, as to the larger part, of such as were Christians only in name, unworthy of regard in the divine estimation, and for this reason forbidden to be comprehended within the sacred inclosure, marked out by the *reed* [q] or measure of St. John.

The visions hitherto adduced have all been objective to the corrupt or idolatrous state of Christianity; the three, which are yet behind, were granted with a contrary design, to depict the circumstances of the chosen few, who should retain their integrity amidst the general depravity of their brethren.

And the first that demands our attention is the Prophesying of Two Witnesses in sackcloth for 1260 days [r]. By these we are to understand the sincere disciples of Christ, who adhere unshaken to the pure word of God, and constantly withstand the reigning superstitions, du-

[q] Rev. xi. 1.   [r] Rev. xi. 3.

ring the whole period in which they are suffered to prevail. They are *two* in number, in allusion to the several pairs of the servants of God in the Old Testament, to whom they are compared; for, like Moses and Aaron in Egypt and in the wilderness, they *smite the earth with plagues*, and send *fire out of their mouth* to *devour their enemies*[s], or denounce the anger of God against the opposers of the true religion; like Elijah and Elishah, who protested against the idolatry of Baal, they have power to *shut heaven, that it rain not in the days of their prophecy*[t], or to withhold the blessings of providence from such as resist their testimony; and like Zorobabel and Joshua in the Babylonish captivity, they are *the two olive-trees, and the two candlesticks standing before the God of the earth*[u], or the great teachers and luminaries of the Church.

[s] Rev. xi. 5, 6. Exod. vii, viii, ix, x. Numb. xvi. 35.   [t] Rev. xi. 6. 1 Kings xvii. 1.
[u] Rev. xi. 4. Zech. iv. 2, 3.

And

SERM. X.

And they prophesy, or preach, *in sackcloth*; because their office is to lament the desertion of their fellow Christians, and to exhort them to repentance; and because they themselves, when about to *finish their testimony*, are to be persecuted and *overcome* of the *Beast*, the Roman power already described, and to be *slain* by it[w]; till at length almighty truth shall prevail, and genuine Christianity shall revive and be exalted, or, as it is expressed in the metaphorical language of this book, their *dead bodies* shall be raised, and they shall *ascend up to heaven*, in the sight of their enemies, *in a cloud*[x].

The same persons, who are here called Witnesses, are adumbrated anew in the vision of a hundred and forty-four thousand, selected out of the twelve tribes of the children of Israel[y]; the tribes of Israel denoting, as in other places of the Revelation, the society of real Christians:

[w] Rev. xi. 7.   [x] Ver. 8. 11, 12.
[y] Rev. xiv. 1. vii. 3, 4.

for

for these are characterized as *virgins*, that is, untainted with idolatry, which, in a figurative sense, is fornication; as *redeemed from among men*, not carried away with the general degeneracy; and *followers of the Lamb wheresoever he goeth* [z], persevering stedfastly in the doctrine of Christ, whilst the rest of the Christian world are enslaved to the worship of the Beast.

Lastly, the forlorn condition of the Church, during the dominion of the *Man of Sin*, which had been described in the two foregoing visions, is again expressed by the flight and abode of the Woman in the Wilderness [a]. The Woman, in this vision, represents the Church of Christ in its purity [b]; and as the Israelites, after they had been delivered from the bondage of the house of Egypt, were carried into the Wilderness, and there miracu-

---

[z] Rev. xiv. 4.
[a] Rev. xii. 1, 2. 5, 6. 13, 14.
[b] See page 275, 276.

SERM. X.

lously supported; so the Christian Israel, after she had escaped the rage of her first enemy, the Dragon, or the persecuting Pagan Emperors, was permitted to make her escape into a similar place of refuge; where she is to be *nourished for a time and times and half a time* [d], that is, for three years and a half, or forty-two months, or 1260 days, the period limited by providence for the prevalence of her adversaries.

Having thus discovered the general signification of the Seven Contemporary Visions of the prophecy of the Open Book; the secret purpose of the two that immediately precede, namely the Inner Court of the Temple, which St. John is ordered to measure [e], and the battle of Michael and the Dragon concerning the Woman ready to be delivered [f], will be easily ascertained. The Inner Court of the Jewish Temple, as opposed to the

[d] Rev. xii. 6. 14.   [e] Rev. xi. 1.
[f] Rev. xij. 3, 4, 5. 7, 8, 9. See page 247.

Outer,

Outer, was appropriated to the Priests and Levites; and Christians under the new covenant being said to be *Priests to God* [g], this Inner Court, measured by the *reed* or rule of the Apostle, must mean the primitive Church, yet unadulterated by human ordinances, and in all respects conformable to the divine word. Not that, even in these times of simplicity, the Christians were totally exempt from troubles; as is shadowed out in the other synchronical vision, in which Michael, the tutelar Angel of the Jews [h], and now the protector of the Christians, contends with and subdues the Dragon, or Heathen Emperors of Rome; after which, the Woman, or Christian Church, is delivered of a *man-child*, or gains a civil establishment among the Gentiles under the protection of Constantine [i].

Besides the Two Visions, which are the immediate antecedents of the Seven

[g] Pet. ii. 5. 9.   Rev. i. 6. v. 10. xx. 6.
[h] Dan. x. 21. xii. 1.   [i] See pages 1. 276, 277.

SERM. X.

beforementioned, there are other Two, which are the immediate subsequents of the same; the effusion of the vials, and the falls of the Beast and of Babylon [k]. It is plain from the text itself, that by the pouring out of the Vials in general is signified the ruin of the antichristian Beast; and that the seven Vials in particular are so many successive degrees of that ruin. But as this part of the Open Book, as well as that which follows, is not yet sufficiently cleared by the completion, I forbear all conjectures concerning it. Our business, in the examination of this obscure volume, is, not to prophesy, but to interpret; not to foretell things before they are fulfilled, but, after they are fulfilled, to illustrate the prediction from the event. From what we now discern of the design and purpose of the Apocalypse, we see enough to direct our practice, and confirm our faith:

---

[k] Rev. xvi. See page 248.

faith: for the rest, we presume not to intrude into *the secret things* which *belong unto the Lord our God*[1], or to penetrate the mysteries of the divine counsels, which he himself has thought fit to envelop, for the present, in thick *clouds and darkness* [m].

II. But the Revelation of St. John includes, together with the Open Book, another volume, containing the prophecy of the Sealed Book [n]; both tomes being synchronical to one another [n], and, as we shall now see, no otherwise differing, than that the one is chiefly concerned in delineating the affairs of the Christian Church, and the other in describing the revolutions of the Roman Empire.

With respect to this latter prediction, it has been observed to you once before [o], that its contents are not related, like

---

[1] Deut. xxix. 29.
[n] See pages 236.—250. 256.
[m] Pf. xcvii. 2.
[o] See page 239.

those

those of the open book, in different sets of contemporaneous visions, but follow one another in an exact and regular succession; and consequently, that the events foretold are to come to pass in the same train as the several parts of the prophecy are recorded in the book itself. By examining therefore, and in the order they lie, the constituent portions of this volume, and comparing them, as we go along, with those visions of the little tome, to which they correspond; we shall obtain a general view of the varying fortunes of the Church and Empire, from the first foundation of Christianity to the present times.

The Sealed prophecy is divided into seven periods, denoted by seven Seals. Now it has been proved, that the Six first Seals, in this Book, and the Two Visions of the Inner Court and of the victory of Michael over the Dragon, in the Open Book, are comprehended in one

one and the fame fynchronifm [q]. But the Two Visions in the Open book, it hath been also shewn [r], are both to be interpreted of the Christian Church, whilst free from idolatrous rites, and struggling with the persecutions of the Pagan Emperors: whence it follows, that, in order to elucidate the Six first Seals in the Sealed book, we are of necessity confined to such facts in history, as are to be found in the three first centuries of the Christian æra, or concur with the times of Rome Pagan.

Now it is certain, from undoubted monuments of antiquity, that within the period here assigned there was a series of events that befell the Roman Empire, which answers with great propriety to the characters attributed to these Six Seals. What can better describe the genius of the Christian religion, triumphing over the idol-divinities of Heathenism, and spreading itself, through

---

[q] See page 255.
[r] In the present Lecture: See pages 304, 305.

the ministry of the Apostles, to the remotest corners of the world, than the representation of the person and dignity of Christ, which is given in the first Seal? who is pourtrayed with a *bow*, and riding on a *white horse*, the usual ensigns of war and victory, *and a crown was given unto him, and he went forth conquering and to conquer* [s]. What can more fitly denote the wars between the Jews and Romans, in the reigns of Trajan and Adrian, and the misfortunes which overtook these two inveterate enemies of the cross of Christ, than the symbols of the second Seal, which is distinguished by slaughter and *the taking of peace from the earth* [t]? Or what more strictly correspond to the want and famine that prevailed through the Roman provinces under the family of the Antonines, and to the methods by which this great evil was mitigated, if not removed, by the care of Septimius Severus, eminent in story for

[s] Rev. vi. 1, 2.   [t] Ver. 3, 4.

the equitable administration of his government; than the figure of the person in the third Seal, who is seen riding on a *black* horse, the known colour for distress, and holding in his hands a *Balance*, with which to weigh out to his subjects, in scanty but just proportion, the necessaries of life [u]? The next affliction, that befell the Empire, was the united miseries of war and sickness, in the times of Decius, Gallus, and Valerian: and these are signified in the fourth Seal, where Death is personified, riding on a *pale* horse, and preceded by his four harbingers, or, as they are called by Ezekiel [w], the *four sore judgments* of God, *the sword and the famine and the noisome beast and the pestilence* [x]. To this calamity was subsequent a new and barbarous persecution, which befell the Christians by the order of Diocletian; of which, as might be expected, we are forewarned in the fifth

[u] Rev. vi. 5, 6.   [w] Ezek. xiv. 21.
[x] Rev. vi. 7, 8.

Seal, whose distinguishing note is an *Altar, having under it the souls of them that were slain for the word of God*[y]. Within no long time after this trouble, the Roman government itself underwent a change, yet more extraordinary than any before related; the nature of which is with wonderful exactness declared, in the sixth Seal, by the symbol of *a great earthquake*[z], the constant figure, both in the Old Testament and the New, to denote the ruin of kingdoms, and revolutions of states; and therefore the fittest to represent the commotions that happened in the Empire in the days of Constantine the Great, by whom Paganism was finally abolished, and the Christian religion erected in its place.

From the account here given it appears, that the Six first Seals of this prophecy were intended to mark so many notable events of the Roman Empire, in its Pagan or unconverted state; ac-

[y] Rev. vi. 9, 10, 11.   [z] Ver. 12—17.

cording as these were permitted to promote or retard the interests of the Christian religion, then just beginning to illuminate a benighted world. In the mean while, a way was prepared, through the care of providence, for the gradual publication of the gospel; which, after being long nurtured in the school of persecution, was enabled by the superior power of its truth to conciliate and convert its opposers, and at length, under the auspices of Constantine, to establish itself, in prosperity and purity, throughout the provinces of the Roman Empire.

But the days of restored tranquillity were soon obscured by new clouds of sorrow. For the Church, secure of a stable settlement in the Empire, now become Christian, and having no longer to contend with enemies from without, began, according to the usual tendency of human affairs when destitute of a divine direction, to teem with disorders from within. And although in these times

SERM. X.

times of degeneracy there were never wanting a few upright Christians, who like living embers kept the dying ashes from being quite extinguished (as is intimated in the vision, interposed between the sixth and seventh Seals, of the Virgin-company of a hundred and forty-four thousand [a]); yet the greater part, but too visibly, departed soon and wide from the original terms of the gospel-covenant, and deflected from the strait way that leadeth unto life into the oblique paths of idolatry and superstition. This miserable state is foretold in a variety of apposite and affecting emblems in the Seven Contemporary Visions, so often mentioned, of the Open Book: and the same unhappy appearance of things, together with the calamities which at the same period of time were suffered to desolate the Roman government both in the East and West, is again delineated in that part

[a] Rev. ch. vii.

of the Sealed Book we are now to consider, the Seventh, or last, Seal.

That Seventh Seal, we must here repeat, is distributed into seven portions, each noted by the sounding of a Trumpet [b]; and six of those Trumpets contemporize with the Seven Synchronical Visions, before enumerated, of the Open Book [c]: but the Seven Visions, as has been already proved, are all to be explained of events falling within the times of Papal or Antichristian Rome; and therefore the Six Trumpets must also be interpreted of events coincident with the same times.

Now here again, by examining with attention those parts of the Roman history, which immediately followed the great revolution in religion, mentioned above; we shall find a sufficient variety of well-attested facts, that correspond to the prophetical descriptions, comprehended in the remaining part of this sealed volume.

[b] See page 238. [c] See page 252, 253.

SERM. X.

The chief and memorable affliction, with which the Romans were visited after the reign of Constantine, was the irruption of the Goths and Vandals and other barbarians into the Latin or Western Empire: and the most striking circumstances, with which this amazing desolation was accompanied, from the beginning to the end of it, are recorded in the Four first Trumpets of the Seventh Seal. The sounding of the First Trumpet is followed with *Hail and Fire* cast upon the *Earth* [d]: which has been explained of the first incursion of the Northern nations, who fell at once like a hail-storm on the most fertile of the Roman territories, spreading ruin and destruction as they came, towards the end of the fourth century, after the death of Theodosius the Great. At the sounding of the Second Trumpet a *burning Mountain* is cast into the *Sea* [e]: preluding, as is supposed, to the besieging and burning

[d] Rev. viii. 6, 7.   [e] Ver. 8, 9.

of Rome by Alaric, general of the Goths. When the Third Trumpet founds, a *Star* falls upon the *Rivers* [f]: and this type was verified, when Genferic, the Vandal, invaded the Roman provinces, and the great body of the Empire was fhared into ten feparate kingdoms, according to the exprefs predictions of Daniel and St. John. In the Fourth Trumpet the hiftory of the Latin Empire is carried on to its extinction: this is prefigured by an *Eclipfe of the Sun, Moon, and Stars,* darkening the Roman firmament [g]; and was then fulfilled, when all remaining authority at Rome was fubverted, and the Imperial City, no longer the Queen of Nations and Miftrefs of the World, was reduced to an inferior dukedom, and fubjected to the new Exarchate, erected at Ravenna.

By thefe fteps the Latin or Cæfarean government, or *that which letted,* was

[f] Rev. viii. 10, 11.   [g] Ver. 12.

taken

taken out of the way[h]; and what is of more importance to remark, by the same degrees as the Imperial power thus sunk to its depression, the Papal found means to rise to the opposite point of exaltation. But our present employment is not so much to advert to the methods by which the Roman Pontiff advanced to dominion, as to pursue the sequel of calamities, which, after the fall of the Western Empire, desolated the Eastern, or that of the Greeks. And for a description of these, we must have recourse to the following Trumpets, distinguished, on account of the duration and kind of those calamities, by the name of *Woes*[i].

The most remarkable event, subsequent to the demolition of the Western government, was the sudden rise of the Arabians or Saracens; who, seduced by the great impostor Mahomet, over-ran and harrassed the Roman territories in the East. And to these ravagers the characters of

[h] 2 Thess. ii. 7.   [i] Rev. viii. 13.

the

the Fifth Trumpet, or first Woe [k], have been shewn to answer. The false prophet himself is typified by a *Star fallen from heaven* [l]: *the key of the bottomless pit*, where Satan and his evil angels are bound [m], is *given* to him; which pit being opened by this grand deceiver, *a smoke*, or false religion, issues from it; *and out of* the *smoke Locusts come upon the earth* [n]. This species of animals is employed in the Old Testament to signify the people, who invaded the Israelites from the East [o]; and is therefore fitly used in this place for the Saracens, who attacked the Romans in the same quarter of the globe. They have power to *torment* mankind for a certain season, but not to *kill* them [p]; which was literally the case with the Arabian conquests here foretold: and their victories are ascribed

[k] Rev. ix. 1—13.
[l] Rev. ix. 1.
[m] Rev. xx. 1, 2, 3.
[n] Rev. ix. 2, 3.
[o] Judges vii. 12.
[p] Rev. ix. 5.

to their skill in fighting [q], which was notoriously the manner in which the religion of Mahomet was propagated through the world.

To the Saracen Empire succeeded the Tetrarchies or four Sultanies of the Turks; by whom the Grecian or Eastern government was totally destroyed. These are emblematized in the Sixth Trumpet, or second Woe, by *four Horsemen loosed from Euphrates* [r]; which river was the eastern boundary both of the land of promise, and of the Roman dominions, and from whence the Turks or Ottomans, passing over into Europe, were made the instruments of divine vengeance to punish the Christians for their idolatry. I have had occasion to mention in another place [s], that the Sixth Trumpet in this sealed volume coincides with the Seven Vials in the open book, by the pouring out of which the tyranny of the Beast is to be brought to its end: and as

[q] Rev. ix. 7, 8, 9.   [r] Ver. 13—21.
[s] See page 255, 256.

that

that Beast still exists, though with evident marks of a decline, we must wait, for the further clearing of this part of the Revelation, till Time, the great expounder of prophecy, shall help us to a discovery. Thus much however we may perceive at present of the general design both of this, and of the next or Seventh Trumpet, that they were intended to inform us, the day will surely come, when the yet remaining power of the Beast shall be totally dissolved, and, all the enemies of the true religion being removed, *the kingdoms of this world shall become the kingdoms of Christ*, and *He shall reign for ever and ever* [t].

III. And now to look back, and recapitulate, in few words, the substance of what has been said concerning the Apocalyptic visions. We may observe, that the Revelation of St. John was intended to exhibit, in one uninterrupted strain of symbols, a view of the constitution and

[t] Rev. x. 7. xi. 14, 15.

fates of the Christian Church, through its several periods of propagation, corruption, and amendment, from its beginning to its consummation in glory. In the first of these three periods it is represented in its primeval state of purity, rejecting all communion with the unholy rites of Paganism, and big with the design of converting the world to itself; the enemies that opposed it being the Roman Heathen Emperors. In the second period, now free from external troubles and with the civil powers on its side, it labours with internal maladies; debasing the simplicity of its worship with the invocation of Saints and Images, and persecuting the pious few who dare to reclame against such innovations; whilst in the mean time the Roman Empire itself experiences the anger of offended heaven, first from the irruptions of the barbarous nations in the West, and then from the conquests of the Saracens and of the Turks

Turks in the East. In the third or last period, which is yet future, it is foretold, that the adversaries of the Church of Christ shall be completely subdued; *all the ends of the world shall remember themselves and be turned to the Lord* [u]; the Saints shall rise and reign with Christ; *then cometh the end* [w], even the general resurrection and judgement of mankind; with which catastrophe this majestic scenery is closed.

To the whole scheme of interpretation here given it may be objected, that the symbols throughout the Revelation are so vague and indeterminate, as not to admit of any precise or certain meaning; that in fact the most opposite significations have been affixed to them by different expositors; and consequently, we can have no reasonable assurance that the particular one, which we have espoused, has at all a better claim to be received than any of

[u] Ps. xxii. 27.   [w] 1 Cor. xv. 24.

SERM.
X.

those which have been rejected. But the smallest degree of reflection on the method here pursued, of opening the prophecy before us, will convince you that the objection, in the present case, is of no force. The first thing required in expounding the Apocalypse was to settle with exactness the order and connexion of the constituent parts; and that not by the help of an arbitrary hypothesis, taken up at pleasure, but from principles, existing in the work itself: the next step was to distribute the several visions, agreeably to this arrangement, into different sets, distinguished by the name of Synchronisms. Now the very nature of these Synchronisms requires, that, in looking out for facts to answer them, our search be restrained to particular periods of time, beyond and out of which we are not at liberty to recede. The facts adduced, which happened within those periods, are proved to be genuine from the evidence

of

of unsufpected history: the symbols correspond to the facts; and the facts, in their turn, illustrate the symbols: all which circumstances laid together leave no room to doubt of the soundness and legitimacy of the interpretation derived from them, and exclude the possibility of those precarious and groundless solutions, which have disgraced the systems of former commentators.

The following words, which in their original application were used by the very learned Founder of the present Lecture, in support of his own explanation of the book of Job, are so strictly true of the interpretation, here adopted, of the book of the Revelation, that I cannot better illustrate the superior excellence of that interpretation, than by subjoining them as the best conclusion to these remarks. " The opposers of Mr. Mede " would have done their duty better, and " have given the learned and impartial " public

"public more satisfaction, if, instead of
"labouring to evade two or three inde-
"pendent arguments, they had, in any
"reasonable manner, accounted, How his
"interpretation, which they affect to re-
"present as visionary and groundless,
"should be able to lay open and unfold
"the whole conduct of the Revelation
"upon one entire, perfect, elegant, and no-
"ble plan, which does more than vulgar
"honour to the writer who composed
"it: and that it should, at the same
"time, be as useful in defining the Parts,
"as in developing the Whole; so that
"particular texts, which, for want of
"sufficient light, had hitherto been an
"easy prey to critics from every quarter,
"are now no longer affected by the com-
"mon opprobrium affixed to this book,
"of its being *a nose of wax*, made to suit
"every religious system. All this the
"hypothesis (as it is called) here adopted
"has been able to perform, in a book
              "become,

"become, through time and negligence,
"so desperately perplexed, that com-
"mentators have chosen, as the easier
"task, rather to find their own notions
"in it than to seek out those of the
"author x."

x D. L. Book VI. Sect. ii. at the end.

SERMON XI.

Historical View of the Corruptions of Popery.

ACTS xxvi. 22.

Saying none other things than those, which the Prophets — did say should come.

THE prophecies of Daniel, St. Paul, and St. John, though singly of great weight, receive additional force, if brought near and illustrated by each other. Having already examined them separately and apart, let us now consider them together, and collect the evidence that arises, when they are taken in one view, and form an entire and perfect whole.

From

From the most cursory survey of the three predictions it is evident, that the same scheme and constitution of things, the same persons, events, and times, the origin, continuance, and destruction, of the same tyrannical power (which power by Daniel is noted by the appellation of the *Little Horn*, by St. Paul is denominated the *Man of Sin*, and by St. John is branded with the titles of the *Beast and the False Prophet*) are distinctly foretold in all. If Daniel describes the kingdom, in which the Little Horn was to arise, by such emblems as can belong to none but the Roman [a]; the same emblems, to prefigure the kingdom of the Beast and the False Prophet, are also employed by St. John [b]; from whom we further learn, that his appropriated place of residence is the city of Rome [c]. If Daniel restrains the sovereignty of this Roman power to

[a] Dan. ii. 40—44. vii. 7, 8. 19, 20, 23, 24. xi. 36.
[b] Rev. xiii. 1, 2. 11, 12.
[c] Rev. xvii. 9. 18.

the

the European or Western part of the Empire, after it was divided into ten shares [d]; the same restriction is intimated in one of the Epistles of St. Paul [e], and is more explicitly declared by the beloved disciple in the Apocalypse [f]. If Daniel represents the nature of this usurped dominion as different from every other [g]; St. Paul and St. John instruct us, that this diversity consists in its being a spiritual, not a civil, dominion [h]; which is therefore to be sought for, not in Heathen, but in Christian Rome. If the instances, in which this spiritual dominion is exerted, according to Daniel, be chiefly these, aspiring to supreme and uncontroulable authority over the inhabitants of the earth, affecting divine titles and honours, enjoining the worship of Demons and departed Saints, prohibiting marriage, working false miracles, and persecuting and

---

[d] Dan. vii. 7. 20. 24.   [e] 2 Thess. ii. 6, 7, 8.
[f] Rev. xvii. 12.   [g] Dan. vii. 23, 24.
[h] 2 Thess. ii. 4. Rev. xiii. 11.

killing

killing those who oppose its claims[i]; the same particulars are related, and with new additions and explications, in the writings of St. Paul[k] and St. John[l]. If the duration of this ecclesiastical polity be limited by Daniel to *a time and times and the dividing of time*[m]; the same duration is expressed, and in a variety of phrases, by St. John; by whom the reign of the Beast is fixed to *a time and times and half a time*, or to three years and a half, or *forty-two months*, or *twelve hundred and sixty days*[n]. And lastly, if the demolition of this extraordinary polity be denounced by the prophet of the Old Testament[o]; the same interesting event is promised by the two Apostles of the new[p]. Such a number of coincidencies, all so strange

---

[i] Dan. vii. 8. 20, 21. 25. xi. 36, 37, 38, 39.
[k] 2 Thess. ii. 3—11. 1 Tim. iv. 1—6.
[l] Rev. xiii. 6, 7. 12—17. xvii. 6.
[m] Dan. vii. 25.
[n] Rev. xi. 2, 3. xii. 6. 14. xiii. 5.
[o] Dan. ii. 44. vii. 26.
[p] 2 Thess. ii. 8. Rev. xviii. 2. 10.

and

and unusual in their kinds, to be found in the compositions of three persons, living in different and one in a very remote period, cannot fairly be ascribed to any other cause, than to the impulse of the *self-same Spirit* [q], who *taught them all things* [r], which it was necessary should be communicated for the *admonition* of the Church of Christ, *upon whom the ends of the world* should *come* [s].

But allowing the predictions thus uniformly to agree, a question naturally arises, what proofs are we able to bring, that all, or any of them, have, in some reasonable sense, been fulfilled? This question hath been answered imperfectly already, whilst we were surveying the contents of each prediction by itself: it will now be expedient to discuss the matter at large, and to point out to you the facts, from whence we are led to conclude, that all the prophecies under consideration, as to

[q] 1 Cor. xii. 11.   [r] John xiv. 26.
[s] 1 Cor. x. 11.

the greater part, have, at this very time, received their completion.

Now of the characters, recorded in Scripture as the undoubted marks of Antichrist, *many* at least have been shewn to belong, exclusively, to the tyranny now existing in Papal Rome. For, first of all, this power is certainly a Roman one; secondly, it is confined to the limits of the Latin or Western Empire; thirdly, it arose among the ten kingdoms, into which that Empire was parted by the northern barbarians; fourthly, its throne or seat is in the city of Rome; fifthly, it is a Christian power; and, sixthly, it is discriminated from all others, by being of the spiritual or ecclesiastic kind t. These are circumstances so plainly realized in that part of Christendom which is subject to the Roman pon-

---

t See the eleventh of Bishop Hurd's Sermons on the Prophecies; where the prophetic characters of Antichrist, above described, are shewn, and in a very sa... way, to be fairly applicable to the Church of Rome.

tiff, that it is not poſſible, by any art or ſubtlety of our adverſaries, they can be evaded or denied.

But the grand and deciſive argument to demonſtrate, that the Apoſtaſy of Papal Rome is indeed foretold in the ſacred oracles, is derived from the correſpondence between the ſeveral acts of power aſcribed to Antichriſt in the prophecies, and thoſe claimed and exerciſed by the ruling head of the Roman Communion. Theſe therefore it will be our care to draw out at length, and, without adhering to the ſtrict order of time, to ſpecify the corruptions, in doctrine and worſhip, avowedly introduced by Popery into the ſyſtem of Chriſtianity, by which the ſimpleſt and pureſt of all religions has been diſhonoured, and the ſalutary purpoſes, in great meaſure, obſtructed, for which it was granted by an all-gracious providence to mankind.

1. In the primitive Church, the parity of Biſhops was admitted without exception,

tion, and no one had any pre-eminence over the rest, but what arose from the dignity of the See to which he was elected. On this account the Bishops of Rome, which had so long been the seat of government and the Metropolis of the Western world, were entitled to some degree of respect over and above what was due to prelates of inferior districts; and the same honour was paid to the Bishops of Antioch and Alexandria, as rulers of the earliest of the Christian churches, and afterwards to the Bishops of Constantinople, when the Imperial residence was transferred to that city. But the distinction of rank and precedence, thus tacitly allowed to these four prelates, was not thought to imply a distinction of power and authority: They, with others of their brethren, were equally bound by the laws and edicts of the Emperors; all were alike supposed to have received their function from the appointment of Christ alone, and not from any concessions of the

successor

successor of St. Peter; and when, so early as the third century, the Roman pontiff presumed to domineer above his fellows, the attempt was treated by Cyprian, Bishop of Carthage, with the utmost scorn and indignation.

It fortuned, towards the close of the following century [u], that a law was proposed by Valentinian, and accepted by the unwary prelates in terms of approbation, that all disputes, which might happen to arise among the members of the Episcopal order, should be referred for the hearing of the Bishop of Rome: the reason assigned was, that religious differences might not be carried before profane or secular judges; and probably, the law itself was merely temporary, at least was never designed to extend beyond the suburbicarian provinces, the only ones within the jurisdiction of the Romish See.

[u] About the year 372. See Mosheim's Ecclesiastical History, translated into English by Archibald Maclaine, D. D. vol. I. p. 287. note *n.*

From this circumstance we may date the origin of that spiritual despotism, which the Popes found means to erect, and to which all Europe was induced to conform with an unlimited obedience. It is curious to trace the steps, by which so wonderful an influence over the minds of men was effected.

After the passing of the above law, it became no unusual thing for subordinate prelates, when invaded in their rights, to have recourse for assistance to the Roman pontiff; who, far from displeased at such an application, and always deciding for those who fled to him for protection, took an easy occasion from thence to increase his own authority. The declining state of the Emperors in the West, added to their absence from the Imperial city, was a new opportunity offered to the Popes to govern there without controul: and the quarrels, so famous in history, between the bishops of Rome and Constantinople, the one aiming at supremacy, the other more modestly labouring to preserve his independence, and which did not end but with the total separation of the Latin and Greek Churches, are an ample proof that the same endeavours to gain an ascendance were not wanting in the East. But the accessions of power, hitherto acquired, were much too scanty to satisfy the growing ambition of these ghostly rulers. Not content with the advantages, so fraudulently obtained, over their brethren of the hierarchy, they asserted next that, as visible heads of the church, their authority was superior to that of all synods and councils, whether provincial or general; none of which, it was pretended, could legally be convened, but by their permission; and whose determinations were of no validity, unless inforced and ratified by their sentence. It was an easy step after this to proceed to whatever higher degrees of arrogance they pleased; to assume the disposal of ecclesiastical offices and honours of every kind; to demand an exemption, for themselves, and for all the orders of the clergy, from secular justice; to promote appeals to their own courts; to exalt their own decisions, and those of the canons, above the injunctions of Scripture; and, in a word, to act in all respects as divinely-appointed Monarchs of the Church of Christ. Nothing remained to render the system of tyranny complete, but to exert the same transcendent prerogative over princes and sovereigns, as they already exercised over the bishops and clergy; from the ceremony permitted to them of crowning to infer the right of making kings, of absolving subjects from their allegiance, of trying, condemning and dethroning refractory monarchs, and transferring their sceptres to new masters more subservient to their will: Nor was it long before the ill-judged munificence of the Emperors, on whom till now they had been dependent, enabled them to reach this sublimest pinnacle of

priestly

priestly pride, and, in consequence of a power derived to them from Jesus Christ, to degrade to the lowest acts of humiliation, to excommunicate, and to depose their benefactors. The execution of this last impiety, which had often been meditated before, was kept for the times of the profligate Hildebrand, better known by the name of Gregory VII; whose political discernment and intrepid temper, unchecked by any restraints from moral principles, qualified him in an eminent manner to advance the Papal supremacy to its greatest height. And to this new species of oppression, which was hereafter to have place in the Christian Church, the prophets are thought to prelude; when they hold out to us Antichrist, as having a *mouth speaking great things, and a look more stout than his fellows,* and *thinking to change times and laws* [w]; as *opposing and magnifying himself above all that is*

---

[w] Dan. vii. 20. 25.

called

called God or that is worshiped [x]; and as causing all, both small and great, rich and poor, free and bond, to receive his *mark in their foreheads* [y].

[x] 2 Thess. ii. 4.

[y] Rev. xiii. 16.—Among other appellations, assumed by the Bishop of Rome, that of *Vicar of God* is one; by which hath been usually understood his unwarrantable claim to exercise all those acts of spiritual sovereignty, which are the peculiar province of the Supreme Being. I rather conceive that this title was originally intended, not as significative of honour, but of humility. The term is borrowed from the Roman Law. Slaves, out of the little *peculium* they were allowed to have of their own, very frequently bought another slave, who was subject to them, as they themselves were subject to their proper masters. Such a slave of a slave, or *servus servi*, was called *Vicarius*: so the word is used by Horace,

"Sive VICARIUS est, qui servo paret, uti mos
"Vester ait, seu Conservus." 2 Serm. VII. 28.

and by Martial,

"Esse sat est Servum; jam nolo VICARIUS esse."
Lib. II. Epig. 18.

and, in allusion to this sense, the Pope sometimes condescends to stile himself *Vicarius*, and at other times, *Servus Servorum, Dei* &c. Both expressions are synonymous, and one of them explains the other.

2. The Redeemer of mankind, before he ascended to heaven from whence compassion to a miserable world had brought him down, delivered to his disciples a Rule of Faith, which was by them committed to writing in the New Testament, and by which the most ordinary capacity may be furnished with that wisdom that will make him *wise unto salvation* [z]. To this rule, which in the strictest sense may be called infallible, we Protestants profess solely to adhere; so that whatever proposition is not, either expressly, or by fair and logical consequence, deduced from it, ought not of necessity to be made an article of a Christian's creed. But a rule, so direct as this, was but little suited to the crooked politics of the church of Rome: which therefore, in defiance of a positive command [a], has added to the doctrines of God's book a long list of others, handed down, as is alleged, by Tradition,

---

[z] 2 Tim. iii. 15.
[a] Deut. xii. 32. Rev. xxii. 18, 19.

through a course of seventeen hundred years, and to be received with the same reverence as holy Scripture. If it be asked, how are we to know that these traditional doctrines have, none of them, been changed or mutilated, in passing through so many hands; we are answered, they have always been admitted as genuine by the judgement of the Catholic Church, and that judgement, in matters of faith at least, is infallible. If we go on to ask, in what part of the Catholic Church this same infallibility resides; some of their writers tell us, it is in the Pope, others in a general council, a third sort, in the Pope and a general council together; whilst others maintain, that it is diffused through all the members of the Romish communion, and others again, that it exists in the collective body of Christians, wherever situated in the world. When Protestants are urged for a *reason of the hope that is in them*[b], they refer with

[b] 1 Pet. iii. 15.

confidence

confidence to the written word, which is the only authorized standard of theological truth, and comprehends whatever is required from a Christian either to believe or do. When Papists to this original and all-sufficient rule would add another, derived from Tradition, which they recommend to us as more complete, and also as infallible; we reply, that all Tradition is uncertain in its nature; and on the boasted quality of infallibility we can have no reliance, since the very Church, which claims to be in possession of it, has never yet been able to determine where it is to be found.

If the Church of Rome be thus culpable in arrogating to itself Infallibility, it is equally to be blamed for assuming another divine attribute, the Forgiveness of Sins. The conditions, on which this invaluable privilege was granted to those, who were converted from a state of heathenism to Christianity, were *Repentance toward God, and Faith toward our Lord Jesus*

Jesus Christ[c]; as to such as are already professed Christians, and through infirmity or surprize have fallen from their integrity, they are Faith and renewed Obedience for the future. To publish these offers of mercy to an unbelieving and guilty world, was the great business of the Apostles' ministry; when, in virtue of a commission from their Lord and Master, they went forth, *preaching peace by Jesus Christ*[d], and proclaimed to Jew and Gentile the glad tidings of that religion, according to the terms of which, as then declared by them *on earth*, every man's sentence, whether of acquittal or condemnation, would be finally decided *in heaven*[e]. Further power of absolving and retaining sins the Apostles themselves had not; and we have no reason to conclude that greater authority in so important a point is conferred on their less enlightened successors. Yet the Church of Rome,

[c] Acts xx. 21.   [d] Acts x. 36.
[e] Matth. xvi. 19. John xx. 23.

with

with a boldness that is beyond conception, has dared to alter the original conditions of acceptance promulged in the New Testament, and to impose others of its own, of which it is hard to say whether they be more repugnant to sense or honesty. Instead of that pious sorrow, which flows from the love of God and *worketh repentance to salvation not to be repented of* [f], they have substituted what they call Attrition, or the servile fear of punishment, accompanied with Absolution, if it can be had, as sufficient for the remission of the greatest guilt. Instead of that amendment of life, which both Scripture and reason affirm is the one thing needful to regain the favour of our offended maker, they teach that Confession to a Priest, together with an arbitrary penance injoined by him, is of ample merit to atone for the breaches of the moral law. In derogation of the purifying efficacy of the *blood of Christ*, which,

[f] 2 Cor. vii. 10.

as the Apostle speaks, *cleanseth us from all sin* [g], and discharges all its stains, they pretend that souls in a separate state are purged from the defilements contracted here, by the fire of a fabulous Purgatory. And by the scandalous doctrine, that pardon for every iniquity, whether committed or designed, may be purchased for money, and the more scandalous practice of exposing Indulgences to open sale, they have evacuated the obligations to that *holiness, without which no man shall see the Lord* [h]. Who now that reflects on such an impious invasion of the prerogative belonging to God alone, and at the same time remembers what is said in the *sure word of prophecy* [i] of the great corruption which was to happen in aftertimes in the Church of Christ, can help being persuaded that the instances now adduced were principally in the minds of the inspired penmen, when they describe

[g] 1 John i. 7. [h] Heb. xii. 14.
[i] 2 Pet. i. 19.

Antichrist as *speaking marvellous things against the God of Gods* [k]; *sitting as god in the Temple of God, shewing himself that he is god* [l]; and *opening his mouth in blasphemy against God, to blaspheme his name* [m]?

3. No sooner had the Christians emerged from a state of persecution under the Heathen Emperors, than comparing, as was natural, their present and past conditions, they were led to contemplate with an uncommon degree of approbation the characters of those holy men, who by the purity of their lives and the constancy of their sufferings even unto death had given the most honourable attestation to the truth and excellence of their religion, and had been the instruments of procuring for them much of the peace and security they now enjoyed. Gratitude, affection, every virtuous movement of the mind, concurred to promote so just an esteem for persons so highly deserving; and many

[k] Dan. xi. 36.   [l] 2 Thess. ii. 4.
[m] Rev. xiii. 6.

were incited to emulate such glorious examples, and to *be followers of them who through faith and patience inherited the promises*[n]. But the confines of right and wrong, like those of light and shade, are separated by narrow and almost imperceptible limits; and from a due regard to an extravagant veneration the transition was too easy. The Fathers of the fourth century, instead of moderating this growing evil, inflamed it by their indiscretions. The tombs of the primitive Christians were chosen, as fit places for the exercises of devotion: the graves, where their bodies had been deposited, were sought with an over-curious diligence: visions and revelations were called in to discover their relics, which were preserved with the most anxious care, as never-failing remedies against the power of evil spirits and natural diseases; and as the Gentiles from honouring their Heroes exalted them into Demons or inferior divinities,

[n] Heb. vi. 12.

vinities, so Christians, from the same principle of superstition, operating in similar circumstances, advanced their Martyrs into heaven, and invoked them as the bestowers of present and future blessings. All these errors were fostered and encreased by the bigotry of the Church of Rome; in which real Angels and fictitious Saints are equally addressed, as patrons and advocates of mankind; and the intercession of the Virgin Mary in particular is supplicated, as even more available than that of her *holy child Jesus*[o]: Among other instances of unlawful adoration, invented by the same idolatrous society, we may reckon here that most shocking and absurd one, which is paid to the bread and wine in the celebration of the Eucharist: this practice was originally begun on an opinion, first conceived by an enthusiast of the ninth century, that the elements after consecration are transubstantiated, or changed into the

[o] Acts iv. 27.

body and blood of Chrift; and fuch a doctrine, however pofitively contradicted by the palpable teftimony of fenfe, being calculated to infpire ideas of awe and horror, which are always wanted in a falfe religion, was erected in the thirteenth century into an article of faith, not to be refufed under pain of damnation. The Form of worfhip was equally reprehenfible with the Objects of it. Images and pictures of thofe, who had acquired the fame of a fingular piety, were early made, and almoft as early looked up to as animated with the prefence of the perfons whom they refembled: and although this fpecies of religious homage was oppofed, and with various fuccefs, for 120 years, it afterwards obtained the fanction of the fecond council of Nice, and has been continued fince, without interruption, among the votaries of the Papal See. It is fuperfluous to add, that all the obfervances, mentioned here, are not only not commanded in Scripture, but are in direct

direct violation of it; inconsistent with the services we owe to God, even the Father, and irreconcileable with that exclusive regard we are enjoined to pay to the mediation of his Son. Yet, unscriptural and forbidden as they are, they were distinctly foretold many ages ago by the holy prophets, when they represent the Apostasy of *the latter times* as consisting in *honouring, together with* the true God, *Mahuzzim*, that is, Angels and departed Saints; in *giving heed to seducing spirits and doctrines concerning Demons;* and *causing the earth, and them which dwell therein, to make an Image to the Beast* [p].

4. The same spirit of superstition, which produced an idolatrous veneration of the Martyrs, discovered itself in another and a more extraordinary way. The Roman republic, among other useful institutions, proposed rewards and honours for the

[p] Dan. xi. 38, 39.   1 Tim. iv. 1.   Rev. xiii. 12. 14, 15.

encourage-

encouragement of lawful Matrimony; and Constantine himself had indirectly favoured this state, by granting the benefits of legitimation to children born in concubinage, provided the parents intermarried afterwards. But the notion, which then began to prevail, of the superior merit of celibacy, induced this Emperor to depart from his own wise maxims, and to repeal the famous Papian Law, enacted by Augustus, for the express purpose of conferring privileges on those who were the parents of a numerous offspring. The Christians, already deeply tinctured with fanaticism, eagerly adopted the ideas of the reigning prince; and, deprived of the opportunity of displaying their zeal by dying for the cause of Christ, were fond of inflicting voluntary sufferings on themselves. In order to cultivate a more intimate communion with God, multitudes of both sexes retired into caves and desarts, where, abandoning all human connections, they devoted themselves

selves to a rigorous poverty and a single life. These principles and practices were nothing more at first than the genuine effects of simple superstition: but the Roman pontiff, with his wonted subtlety, took advantage of the ruling weakness, and converted it into one of the most powerful engines to extend his own dominion. That crafty prelate was too sensible not to perceive, that the chief circumstance, which attached the Clergy to secular concerns, was the love they bare their children and families; and that nothing was more likely to subdue them to an entire conformity to his will, than depriving them of this object of affection, and engaging them solely to the interests of their own order. To promote this design, the most extravagant praises were lavished on a single life; which was recommended as highly laudable in all, and urged as the indispensable duty of those who by their office were obliged to an exemplary purity, and admitted to a nearer intercourse

intercourse with heaven. This masterstroke of policy was effected, in the eleventh century, by the intrigues of Gregory VII. when, in spite of the propensities of nature, in spite of the plainest directions of Scripture, which commends the state of Marriage in general as *honourable in all* [q], and gives particular precepts concerning that of Bishops, Presbyters, and Deacons [r], the primary command of providence was blasphemously infringed, and an inviolable celibacy was imposed on all the orders of the Clergy. But thus it was, that the spirit of prophecy had before declared; by which we are taught, that the same antichristian power, which should injoin the worship of demons, should also *not regard the desire of women* [s], and that, among other abominable doctrines introduced by him, this of *forbidding to marry* [t] should be one.

[q] Heb. xiii. 4.   [r] 1 Tim. iii. 2. 11. Tit. i. 6.
[s] Dan. xi. 37.   [t] 1 Tim. iv. 3.

5. The

5. The religion of Jesus, like that of Moses, was established by signs and wonders; which are the proper credentials of a revelation coming from God, and were attended with all those characters of truth, which the most scrupulous enquirer could demand. They were exhibited in public, before enemies and friends, in a learned and inquisitive age, and on the most eminent theatre in the world: they were employed in confirmation of doctrines worthy of God, and of the utmost importance to mankind: they were accompanied with no appearances of vanity or ostentation, and brought no gain or advantage to the performers; and all of them are attested by persons, who gave the most decisive proofs of their integrity, by chusing rather to dye than deny them. On this footing the evidence for the gospel-miracles stands; and the testimony, which establishes them, is so circumstanced, that " its falshood would even be more miraculous than the miracles

racles it relates;" so that, by the confession of scepticism itself [u], the most *academic faith*, without incurring the disgrace of credulity, may ⟨give⟩ them its assent. The religion of ⟨pa⟩pal Rome also boasts its prodi⟨gies⟩ and of the most astonishing kind: but instead of recommending themselves to the belief of a sober examiner, they bear about them the plainest indications of fraud and folly. Many have been detected by contrary evidence; many detect themselves by their absurdity: some are related by suspicious persons; others are wrought for suspicious purposes, to sooth the errors or subserve the interests, of a party: and, besides the innate marks of falshood with which they abound, they are of that very sort, which are recorded in Scripture as clear and unerring notes of Antichrist: for thus it is, that this *son of perdition* is pourtrayed by St. Paul and St. John: *whose coming is after the working of Satan, with all power and*

[u] See Mr. Hume's Essay on Miracles.

signs

signs and lying wonders, and deceivableness of unrighteousness in them that perish: and he doth great wonders, and deceiveth them that dwell on the earth, by means of the Miracles which he hath power to do[w].

6. But we have not yet attained the complete idea of Popish pravity. For when now the Roman pontiff had worked his way to a supremacy, unknown and unallowed in the Church of Christ, and on the strength of that supremacy had proudly arrogated divine honours; when he had contaminated the purity of the Christian faith by the worship of idol-mediators, and trampled on the rights of humanity by an unnatural and un-commanded celibacy; and to all these instances of corruption had added the illusive arts of pretended miracles; then it was, that he filled up the measure of his guilt, by exerting his ill-gotten power to the horrid purposes of

[w] 2 Thess. ii. 3. 9, 10. Rev. xiii. 13, 14.

Persecution. This last contrivance, the opprobrium of human nature as well as of revealed religion, though permitted to disgrace other communities, was no where reduced to a system but in the Church of Rome: and there indeed we find the principles of this system laid open, and exemplified in all their dreadful forms; sometimes occasionally, in the cruelties exercised towards those faithful *Witnesses* [x], who refused to *worship the image of the Beast* [y], and more professedly, in that infernal tribunal, the Inquisition. Here again, as the sacred prophets have condescended to notice other parts of this extraordinary character, we are the less to wonder, if this, the finishing one, be particularly described; first by Daniel, where the *Little Horn makes war with the Saints and wears them out and prevails against them* [z]; and afterwards by St. John, where

---

[x] Rev. xi. 3.   [y] Rev. xiii. 15.
[z] Dan. vii. 21. 25.

SERM. XI.

Babylon, the Mother of Harlots, is *drunken with the blood of the Saints, and with the blood of the martyrs of Jesus* [a].

It may be thought, that the errors here objected to Popery, to which a variety of others might have been subjoined [b], were introduced by Popes, whose private vices were as flagitious as their public government was tyrannical. But the truth is, that all the Roman Bishops, from the reign of Constantine, uniformly laboured to extend their jurisdiction, and with unrelaxing perseverance carried on the same scheme. The hands, which held the reins of empire, were changed; but the spirit, which guided them, was the same. Every new pontiff adopted the schemes of his predecessor; and one encroach-

[a] Rev. xvii. 6. xviii. 24.

[b] The reader, who wishes to see a Recapitulation of the Prophecies relating to Popery, may do well to consult the twenty-sixth Dissertation of the learned Bishop of Bristol, in the third Volume of his very useful Dissertations on the Prophecies.

ment was still succeeded by another, till at length the fabric of superstition was perfected, and towered above the clouds.

And here, by way of conclusion, we may observe, that all endeavours to effect a reconciliation with the Church of Rome must ever be vain and fruitless. Such a comprehension, even upon the moderate plan that has been proposed by Grotius and some others, is absolutely impossible. The Roman communion, by its absurd pretences to infallibility, has precluded itself from receding from any of its most obnoxious tenets; and Protestants, from the very nature of their principles, are incapable of making any concessions. *What fellowship hath righteousness with unrighteousness? and what communion hath light with darkness? And what concord hath Christ with Belial? and what agreement hath the Temple of God with Idols? Wherefore*

SERM. XI.

fore come out from among them, and be ye separate, saith the Lord, and touch not the unclean thing; and I will receive you; and I will be a Father unto you, and ye shall be my sons and daughters, saith the Lord Almighty [c].

[c] 2 Cor. vi. 14, 15, 16, 17, 18.

SERMON XII.

The Reformation vindicated from the objections of the Romanists.
CONCLUSION.

Rev. xviii. 4.

Come out of her, my people; that ye be not partakers of her sins, and that ye receive not of her plagues.

THE errors of the Romish Church, enumerated in the last Lecture, though gradually increasing from the times of Constantine, did not arrive at their height, till the thirteenth century; at which period, the Papal usurpations were carried to their utmost length, and true religion was obscured and well nigh lost amidst the prevailing interests of vice and superstition.

superstition. Some feeble attempts to resist such exorbitant claims, and to restore the genuine doctrines of the gospel to their pristine splendor, had indeed been repeatedly made, by different persons, in different parts of the world: of whom the Waldenses and the Albigenses in the twelfth century, Wickliff, father of the Lollards, in the fourteenth, and Huss, with his companion, Jerome of Prague, in the fifteenth, are deservedly reckoned among the chief. But the honour of tearing off the mask, which had so long concealed the horrors of this corrupt communion, and of exposing its deformity to open view, was reserved for the sixteenth century, and for the daring hand of Luther. That intrepid reformer, it is well known, began his attack on the Romish hierarchy with denying the extravagant merit then generally attributed to Indulgences: and the detection of one abuse conducting him, insensibly, to that of a second and a third, he found, the more

he

he examined into the tenets of Popery, the less defensible they appeared; till at length, to his own surprize no less than that of others, he was compelled to question the Infallibility, so confidently claimed by the sovereign head of this depraved society; the distinguishing principles of which, he was now convinced, were not more opposed to those of primitive Christianity, than repugnant to the dictates of sound reason.

The boldness of Luther's preaching, not being disgraced by any defects in his moral character, made, as was to be expected, a deep impression on his hearers; nor was it long, before his opinions were divulged, and with an astonishing rapidity, from Saxony and Germany, to all the parts of Europe. But, besides the force of religious motives, there were other causes, which at that time concurred to spread the new doctrines, and to which their quick and surprising progress may justly be ascribed. Of these, the revival of learning abont the fame period, and the art of printing, invented not long before, were by no means the leaft. Copies of the Scriptures, together with the writings of the controverfialifts, being now multiplied, they were perufed with an uncommon avidity, as well by the vulgar and illiterate, as by the rich and learned: and the minds of men, awakened from that lethargy, in which they had flumbered for fo many ages, were prepared for pufhing their enquiries into a wider fphere, and qualified to judge of the frauds and abfurdities of the ancient fyftem. Political confiderations lent their aid to thefe natural advantages. The remarkable fchifm of the Antipopes, which had prevailed in the two preceding centuries, for fifty years, had a great effect in diminifhing the reverence to the Romifh See: the libertinifm of many of the reigning Pontiffs, and of the higher orders of churchmen, promoted ftill further the growing averfion: the immenfe wealth, with its neceffary necessary attendant, excessive power, accumulated by the Popish clergy; their extensive immunities, added to their numerous and oppressive encroachments on the privileges of the laity; were so many new incitements to princes to recover the possession of those vast revenues, which the mistaken piety of their ancestors had lavished on the ecclesiastics, and of which they themselves had been so long deprived. All these causes, which singly had great weight, could not but operate with increasing strength, when united; and are to be regarded by serious men as purposely combined by providence, in order to secure the truth and purity of religion, and produce a revolution in the sentiments of mankind, the most extraordinary, as well as the most beneficial, that has happened since the first publication of the gospel [d].

[d] See the History of the Emperor Charles V. by Dr. Robertson, Book II. where the curious reader may be gratified with an accurate inquiry into the causes which contributed to the progress of the Reformation.

The

SERM. XII.

The Reformation, thus auspiciously begun by Luther, was attended with another circumstance, which, for its importance, deserves to be particularly adverted to. As this bold sectary advanced in the study of theology, to which he now addicted himself with unwearied diligence, he was not only more and more persuaded of the degeneracy of the Romish Church, but he discovered also that this degeneracy had been plainly foretold in Scripture; that the character of Antichrist, so largely there described, was verified in the Roman pontiff; and, as the natural result of such a discovery, that every sincere believer was under an absolute necessity of withdrawing from his communion. This was a consequence, of which Luther at first was not in the least aware; for, far from having any intention to disclaim the supremacy of the Apostolic see, he professed the most implicit submission to its authority, and for some time had not the smallest doubt of its divine original. But when he found, by a careful comparison of facts and prophecies, that the corruptions, then actually existing in the Church of Rome, were the very same with those declared in the inspired oracles; and reflected also, that the warning voice, which had proclaimed these delusions of Antichrist, had commanded the faithful people of God to renounce the society of this impostor[e]; the conclusion was unavoidable, that all persons, who were persuaded that Papal Rome was indeed concerned in the sacred predictions, had not only the choice, in point of right, but were obliged, in point of duty, to separate themselves from a Church, whose communication was infectious, and in which they could no longer continue, without *partaking of its sins*[e].

On this ground then, that the Pope was Antichrist, the great secession of Pro-

[e] Rev. xviii. 4.

testants was begun; and on this ground the lawfulness of such a secession may be clearly shewn. For although to forsake the external communion of a Church, where there is no urgent necessity for such a procedure, be without excuse; yet, when a separation must either be made, or we must participate with others in matters which appear to us to be sinful, no reasonable man can have any scruples, as to the part he ought to take. Not every separation then from the Church, but a causeless separation only, is to be condemned: and the true reason, why Protestants hold themselves bound to leave the society of Papists, is not so much because the latter are known to maintain errors in doctrine and to have introduced corruptions in worship, which the former disavow; but because they impose these errors and corruptions upon others, and have so ordered the terms of Church-fellowship, that we must join with

with them in these things, or in nothing. This it is, which fixes the mark of Antichrist on the Church of Rome, and renders it unsafe and unallowable for Christians of other denominations to unite with it in matters of religion. The imputation of schism therefore, fall it where it will, lights not justly upon us: the danger and the punishment, annexed to such a crime, it becomes *them* more particularly to consider, who have made it impracticable for others to associate with them, by requiring unlawful conditions of communion.

Still however it may be said, as it hath been said, that although to depart from the Romish Church might not, strictly speaking, be schismatical, to have continued in it would at least have been the safer way. For both Protestants and Papists are agreed, that salvation may be had in the Church of Rome; but Protestants only allow it may be had in the

Churches of the reformed; the safer part therefore would have been, to adhere to that society, in which, by the confession of both sides, salvation may be found. If this sophism be intended to operate on any but the most illiterate of the Romish communion, it must surely lose its aim; and few words will suffice to expose its futility.

First then we reply, that it is one of those unfortunate arguments, which, by proving too much, prove, in effect, nothing: for if the principle, on which it is founded, be true, namely, that whatever religion two or more contending parties agree in must therefore be the safest, it will lead us not only to abjure Protestantism, but Christianity also. Thus both Jews and Christians acknowledge the divinity of the religion of Moses; but Christians only acknowledge the divinity of that of Jesus; therefore it is safer to be a Jew than a Christian. Again, unbelievers as well as believers own the truth

truth of natural religion, and believers only own the truth of revealed; therefore natural religion alone ought to be retained, and revelation ought to be rejected. The argument is the same in each of the three cases; and if it concludes nothing in the two latter, why should it be thought to have any force in the former?

Secondly, though Protestants dare not imitate the uncharitableness of Papists, in denying that sincere persons, of all persuasions, whose moral conduct is conformable to their religious knowledge, may be saved; yet both truth and charity oblige them to declare, that the salvation of Papists is not to be obtained but with much difficulty and danger. The doctrines of Popery, if we at all understand their nature, are, in their tendency, destructive both to faith and virtue: how far they, who profess such doctrines, may be answerable for the evil consequences which flow from them, especially in cases where they formally disclaim those consequences, or are hindered, by education or invincible ignorance, from perceiving them, must be left to the unerring decision of Him, who *seeth not as man seeth* [f], and whose *tender mercies are over all his works* [g]. As to others, who have been blessed with opportunities of knowing the *truth as it is in Jesus* [h], yet wilfully shut their eyes against it, and, as far as in them lies, prevent others from seeing it, what their condition will be in another world, neither do we presume to determine; *to their own Master they stand or fall* [i]; all we fear is, that the acceptance of such persons is extremely doubtful, if not quite desperate; and if they are *saved* at all, it must be in the way St. Paul speaks of, only *so as by fire* [k].

Thirdly, granting the premises of this argument to be true, that both sides ac-

---

[f] 1 Sam. xvi. 7.
[g] Pf. cxlv. 9.
[h] Ephef. iv. 21.
[i] Rom. xiv. 4.
[k] 1 Cor. iii. 15.

knowledge a poffibility of falvation in the Church of Rome, and one fide only acknowledges that poffibility in the Churches of the reformed; the conclufion, intended to be drawn from it, that therefore it is fafer to be a Papift than a Proteftant, is demonftrably falfe. For that muft certainly be the fafeft way to falvation, in which there is the greateft fecurity from fin. Now in the controverted points between the Papifts and us, it is not even pretended that for many of them there is any authority in Scripture; on the contrary, if what we fay be true, they are pofitively forbidden and unlawful. By adhering then to the religion of Proteftants, we keep within the letter of the written rule, and fo far are upon fafe ground; and by conforming to the injunctions of Popery, it is a queftionable point at leaft, whether we do not violate the exprefs directions of the divine word. Hence it follows, that the fecurity from finning muft be lefs, and confequently the difficulty

difficulty of obtaining salvation must be greater, in the communion of Papists, than in that of Protestants.

But the emissaries of the Church of Rome, not satisfied with decrying the Reformation itself, have endeavoured in the same fallacious train of reasoning to blacken the characters of those, who effected it; most of whom, it has been alleged, were neither influenced by motives, nor adorned with manners, at all agreeable to the cause they undertook to serve. And so far it is to be lamented, that, with respect to many of these reformers, employment in the service of religion did not exempt them from the common infirmities of human creatures. But this fact, instead of discrediting the work they were engaged in, may be converted into no vulgar argument of the divine goodness. The same providence, which is seen so frequently to direct the crimes and follies of men to promote the great designs of justice in civil life, is equally visible,

visible, when it uses wicked kings and princes as instruments to effectuate its purposes in the religious system. In both cases, an occasion is administered of adoring the correcting hand, that out of partial evil produces universal good, and from means the most disproportionate or faulty can compass ends, subservient in the highest degree to the glory of God, and to the present and future welfare of man.

The same answer will serve for what is further urged against the first reformers in particular, that they understood but very imperfectly the nature of that faith, which they pretended to restore; that the principles, on which they proceeded in the execution of their scheme, were often false, and oftener partial; and that although they might perceive, and with real concern, the abuses which then prevailed, they were none of them possessed of the requisite skill, by which alone those abuses could properly be removed.

And

SERM. XII.

And where is the wonder, if in a case, where no extraordinary assistance was granted or claimed, the persons employed should not at once be able to emancipate themselves from the erroneous notions, to which they had been enslaved? How many salutary regulations in society have originated from wrong conceptions of the nature and end of government, or from the obliquer motives of ambition or avarice in the proposers! And why should either our religious or civil privileges be the less esteemed, supposing them to be real, because both were procured by men, who at first perhaps were not accurately instructed in the true extent of political or Christian liberty? The Reformation, from which we are taught to expect such signal and lasting advantages, cannot, from the nature of it, be accomplished at once, but requires a considerable time in order to its completion; and many of the defects, which attended it in its beginnings, have been gradually remedied in its advancement;

vancement to maturity. The kingdom of Antichrist, whose usurpations it has uniformly opposed, hath already been shaken to its centre; and, if any conjectures of what is future may be formed from what is past, even setting aside the expectations to be derived from prophecy, the power of the Roman pontiff is now upon the wain, and will fill its orb no more.

Conclusion.

The Plan, which I had formed at the entrance on the present course, is now brought to its conclusion: in the prosecution of which I have not confined myself to the minute examination of any single prophet or prophecy, but have laid before you the reasons, from which it may be concluded in general, that there are predictions both of the Old and New Testament, which have been rightly supposed to refer to the defection of Christian Rome. An inquiry of this sort seemed not improperly to precede the accurate and critical investigation of each particular prophecy; a labour, which may well be hoped to engage the attention of future Lecturers, and is indeed the principal object of an Institution, which, more than any other, is calculated to support the cause of Reformed Religion, and which deserves, and will have, the grateful acknowledgments of Protestants, of every community, in the present and in succeeding ages. I have only to add a few short reflections, which may not be without their use to those, to whom they are addressed.

And first, the sober and candid Deist, who has not together with the renunciation of revealed religion thrown off all regards for that which is called natural, may be taught the danger of lightly rejecting a system of faith and practice, such as is proposed by Christianity, and which is recommended by so many circumstances of verisimilitude at least, if not of truth. Nothing, humanly speaking, could be

more

more improbable, than that a religion, so pure and simple as the Christian, so abhorrent from the views of worldly dominion, and so friendly to the liberties of mankind, should become subservient to the worst and most diabolical artifices of ecclesiastic tyranny; unless it be, that, after such a tyranny had been once established, and interwoven in the frame and texture of civil governments, it should again recover its primitive integrity. Yet these are facts so obvious and incontrovertible, as to force themselves on the most incurious observer; and at the same time are so utterly unlike what has happened in the usual course of things, as well as so impossible to be foreseen by the keenest eye of unassisted human sagacity, that the supposition of their making part of a plan, originally settled by the great parent of the universe, and in consequence of that foretold *by the mouth of his holy prophets* [1], is their best and most rational solution.

[1] Acts iii. 21.

Secondly,

Secondly, from hence too the Papist may be convinced that we are not actuated by unworthy motives of real or political aversion, when we refuse to join in communion with the Church of Rome; but by a serious regard to what we conceive to be the will of God, which hath called his *people out of* this spiritual Babylon, that they *be not partakers of her sins, and receive not of her plagues* [m]. Much less need he apprehend, that the revival of a study, which naturally calls to mind the pernicious tendency of the Papal doctrines, has any the most remote intention to awaken the severity of those penal laws, which the exigencies of government and a just regard to our own safety have sometimes made necessary, but which have been so little put in execution, as rather to expose the legislature to the charge of imprudent trifling than of wanton cruelty. *The weapons of our warfare*, like those employed by the first

[m] Rev. xviii. 4.

champions of Christianity, *are not carnal*[n]; and the only arms we wish to employ against him are arguments, proposed in the spirit of love and meekness, and founded on the authority of the same Scriptures, which he holds in common with ourselves.

Lastly, Protestants are above all others concerned to regard with becoming seriousness the prophecies concerning Antichrist, and their completion: as it is on the evidence arising from them, that their own religious principles have been chiefly vindicated, and on which they may be best maintained. But in vain do we express our thankfulness for deliverance from the yoke of Popery, if it be not attended with deliverance from another yoke, not less oppressive and more ignominious, subjection to our vices. A return to the follies of superstition, in these times of improved knowledge, is not much to be feared: our danger now

[n] 2 Cor. x. 4.

arises

arises from the opposite extreme, from licentious principles and degenerate manners; which have well nigh destroyed the reverence that was wont to be paid to civil government as well as to revealed religion, and have given the most serious alarms to every real lover of his country. Whether the state of our morals be so far corrupted, as to render us unfit to be longer entrusted with those advantages, which we have so much abused, is a matter that ought to be well considered by all, who have in any degree contributed to the general depravity. Other nations, like our own, have enjoyed the light of Christianity, and again relapsed into pagan darkness. Such was the case of the Asiatic Churches, to whom St. John addresses the former part of his Revelation; all of whom were once instructed in the saving truths of the gospel, but have since become *the synagogue of Satan*[*], the patrons and promoters of

[*] Rev. ii. 9.

vice

vice and error. The exhortations and threatenings, which were directed by the Spirit of God to them, were meant as warnings to Christians in all ages, who may be in the same or similar circumstances; and the admonition, which was given to the Church of Sardis in particular, is, with equal propriety, applicable to ourselves: *I know thy works, that thou hast a name, that thou livest, and art dead. Be watchful, and strengthen the things which remain that are ready to die; for I have not found thy works perfect before God. Remember therefore how thou hast received and heard, and hold fast, and repent. If therefore thou shalt not watch, I will come on thee as a thief, and thou shalt not know what hour I will come upon thee* [p].

[p] Rev. iii. 1, 2, 3.

THE END.

Lately published by the same AUTHOR; *and sold by* T. CADELL, *in* THE STRAND.

I.

THREE Sermons before the Univerfity of Cambridge, occafioned by an Attempt to abolifh Subfcription to the Thirty-nine Articles of Religion, and publifhed at the Requeft of the Vice-chancellor and Heads of Colleges. The Third Edition.

II.

A Sermon before the Honourable Houfe of Commons, on January 30, 1769.

III.

A Sermon before the Governors of Addenbrook's Hofpital in Cambridge, June 28, 1770.

IV.

An Analyfis of the Roman Civil Law; in which a Comparifon is, occafionally, made between the Roman Laws, and thofe of England: being the Heads of a Courfe of Lectures, publickly read in the Univerfity of Cambridge. The Second Edition.

Lately published by T. CADELL,

TWELVE SERMONS, introductory to the Study of the Prophecies; being the FIRST COURSE preached in Lincoln's-Inn Chapel, at the Bishop of Gloucester's Lecture on this Subject. By Richard Hurd, D. D. Preacher to the Honourable Society of Lincoln's-Inn; and now Lord Bishop of Lichfield and Coventry.

www.ingramcontent.com/pod-product-compliance
Lightning Source LLC
Chambersburg PA
CBHW032016220426
43664CB00006B/264